791.4372

D1578935

PERFORMANCE

## ERRATUM

Page xii, line 25:
*for* 'I have added my own descriptions only where absolutely necessary, and they are set in a different font – e.g., on page 17:'

*read* 'I have added my own descriptions only where absolutely necessary, and they are set in italic.
Descriptions from Cammell's shooting script are set in a different font – e.g., on page 17:'

# PERFORMANCE
## Donald Cammell

*faber and faber*

First published in 2001
by Faber and Faber Limited
3 Queen Square London WC1N 3AU
Published in the United States by Faber and Faber, Inc.,
an affiliate of Farrar, Straus and Giroux, LLC, New York

Photoset by Parker Typesetting Service, Leicester
Printed in England by Clays Ltd, St Ives plc

A CIP record for this book
is available from the British Library
ISBN 0–571–20189–X

2 4 6 8 10 9 7 5 3 1

# CONTENTS

Donald Cammell © 1971, photographed by Myriam Gibril

# INTRODUCTION
## by Professor Colin MacCabe

The notion of a film script is a bizarre and elusive one. In its first manifestation, the attempt to raise the money, the script is a selling document and the prose text that surrounds the dialogue conjures up images, motives and explanations in an attempt to visualize the film for its financiers. In the shooting of the film the script's status varies from director to director: at one extreme an Alfred Hitchcock, determined that every word be followed, every direction observed; at the other a Howard Hawks, for whom the script served as the springboard for every kind of improvisation. Once shot and edited, the film exists in a complexity of colour, lighting, sound, camera angle from which what is then called a script normally extracts little more than the dialogue.

It is probably for this reason that there is no standard and agreed form for the film script – some have little more than dialogue and description, others report some camera angles and movements but not others. None describes the actual image in terms of filters, lenses, colour etc. because the language is either too technical or simply non-existent. In editing this text of *Performance* I have had to confront some first principles of editing, principles complicated by *Performance*'s own extraordinary production history.

*Performance* is a one off: a Hollywood studio picture shot entirely on location and experimenting both with camera and performers. It owes as much to the avant-garde and its emphases as it does to classic Hollywood cinema. It is one of the very rare films that manages to combine both traditions to real effect. It is difficult to imagine any other period of film making when a Hollywood studio would allow a first-time director and producer to make a film with untried actors (only James Fox was an established film star), still less to do it hidden away from the direct supervision of the studio; but in early 1968 when *Performance* was greenlit, Hollywood was willing to try anything. The hammer blows of television competition in the late fifties had been followed by a changing of the guard as the generation of Jack Warner and Harry Cohn retired or died. Hollywood in the late sixties was confronted with a youth culture that it neither knew nor understood and desperate to try anything that might lure alienated youth into the cinemas. To take the single most infamous representative of that generation, Mick Jagger, and put him in a film about sex, drugs and crime must have seemed like a good idea at the time. Jagger, at this period, was a figure of enormous potential significance – the leader of one of the most successful rock bands in the world, but also the victim of one of the most famous drug busts of all time. When police raided Redlands, the country home of Keith Richards, in the summer of 1967 and Jagger and Richards were both arrested and charged for possession of drugs, they transformed the two Rolling Stones from rock stars into generational icons. And the rumours of orgies of unparalleled decadence did little to diminish the image of Jagger as the man all parents warned their adolescent children against.

The exact story of how young American agent Sandy Lieberson persuaded Warners to back his friend Donald Cammell's first-time attempt at film-making may never be told, because none of the participants has the clearest of memories of the period. But it is easy to see how Ken Hyman, who co-owned Warners with his father, might have been tempted by the teaming of Jagger and Fox. He also had a long relationship with Lieberson and trusted him enough to believe that he could handle a first-time director working with an untried cast. In any case the late sixties was one of those rare moments in social history when there was a widespread perception that all the rules were changing; all the bets were off. But if it was in that mood that Warners commissioned the film (and they may have felt that they had added security when Britain's leading cinematographer Nic Roeg joined the team as co-director), they were genuinely shocked by the rushes of the bathroom scene in which drug-taking and deviant sex were simply part of the banal ordinariness of existence. Warners were so outraged that they took the almost unprecedented step of closing the film down. It took all Lieberson's guile to persuade Hyman that the film was under control, and the shutdown only lasted a few days; but from then on the studio had nothing but suspicion for the film, and its history is littered with bizarre scenes including efforts to physically destroy the negative. In the end, under intense pressure from Cammell, who tried to enlist everybody from Kenneth Anger to Stanley Kubrick in his campaign, and after a change of ownership, Warners released the film in the US two years after it had been shot. If they had failed to bury the negative physically, the studio now buried the film in the hottest days of August. The reviews were mixed and the box office minimal; but the story was different when *Performance* opened in London in January 1971.

In Britain *Performance* was a hit both commercially and critically. *Time Out*, unprecedentedly, brought out a special supplement, and the film was immediately recognized as a film that spoke for its time and its generation. Cammell and Roeg had managed to conjure up performances from both actors and camera that made this an immediate milestone in British cinema. It has some claim to be *the* cult film of the seventies. Surprisingly, despite its miserable opening, it achieved this status on college campuses in America as well as in Britain. For a whole generation *Performance* provided a film image to which they could give unqualified assent.

There are five different scripts of *Performance*. The first is a continuous prose text entitled *The Liars* that Donald Cammell, who had just abandoned his first vocation as a painter to try his hand at screenwriting, constructed as a vehicle for Marlon Brando, a man with whom Cammell would try unsuccessfully to make films all his life. Gangster on the run ends up in rock singer's secluded flat – an accurate one line description of *Performance* – also describes this first script. But apart from that narrative kernel, this rather jejune splicing of an American gangster movie on to a 'swinging London' film has little to do with the final film. In the summer of '67, however, Cammell moved to London to write a more professional version of the story set out in conventional script form and based entirely in London. To help him with the sounds and accents of a city in which he had not resided for a decade (he had left London for New York in the late fifties and then moved to Paris with Deborah Dixon at the beginning of the sixties) he enlisted the help of David Litvinoff. There is much pointless argument about who was the real author of *Performance*, Donald Cammell or Nicolas Roeg, the brilliant cinematographer whom Cammell chose as his co-director. The argument is pointless because all the historical records reveal a work of genuine collaboration. But the key role that David Litvinoff played in the genesis of the script is not perhaps generally recognized. Indeed, if the author of the text is the person who uses his own personal experiences as the basis for the

Nicolas Roeg and Donald Cammell

fiction, then Litvinoff has some claim to be the author of the first half of *Performance*. For the gruesomely accurate account of the world of London gangsters in the sixties was drawn from Litvinoff's association with the infamous Krays, and much of the dialogue and the action (down to and including the shaving of the chauffeur's head, a fate which had befallen Litvinoff when he crossed Ronnie Kray) was drawn from the life of this latter day Fagin. Litvinoff came from a large and talented Jewish family that included writers and scholars. But his career was that of a talker and a man of violence. His reputation is of a modern-day Coleridge – no one who ever heard him speak seems to have forgotten the experience. He was homosexual and divided his time between the pinball arcades of Soho, the gambling clubs of Mayfair and the criminal pubs and rough trade of East and South London. He was excited by the violent world of crime and both 'took and dished it out' to use Turner's words about Chas. But he also dabbled in the art world and knew Cammell and his friends. Litvinoff was the figure who moved between the Chelsea set, where Cammell and Jagger were to be found, and the world of East End gangsters. It was his experience and his contacts that provided the figures of the gang boss Harry Flowers and his young performer Chas Devlin. As importantly, it was he who arranged for the Harrow-schooled James Fox to be educated in the accents, dress and style of this world by an ex-boxing-trainer called Johnny Shannon. The casting of the completely untrained Shannon as the central villain is one of the triumphs of the film, but this merely completes a process that began with the collaboration with Litvinoff on the script. The first result of this collaboration was called *The Performers* and gives us a film recognizably like the finished film, particularly in its first half. Whether this second version was pitched to Warner Brothers and then rewritten in the light of their comments, or whether it was revised by Cammell into a more professional shooting script entitled *Performance* and then submitted to Warner Brothers, I have been unable to ascertain. But it is this third version of the text that was issued to all the actors and of which there are multiple copies in existence. I shall refer to this as the shooting script. The first half of this script is, with two crucial exceptions, the film we know. It introduces us to the world of Harry Flowers, the world of protection and performers, of bars and boys, of muscle magazines and guns. But all the stories are, in this third version, told in linear fashion, and the lawyer is not the figure in the courtroom trying to put Harry Flowers in the dock but an upper-class wide boy who thinks he can welsh on his gambling debts. The scene in the shooting script in which Chas follows the lawyer into the Garrick and threatens to cut his tongue out is as pregnant with violence as any of the scenes that remain in the movie. Indeed, one might argue that the naked class antagonism of this scene would have added something to the final film. But Cammell and Roeg had a more important role for the barrister to play. In the finished film he is a crucial narrative device – it is the barrister who threatens to land Harry in jail, or even worse, on the front page of the press. Chas's ultimate sin, which is to bring media attention to bear on the gang, is prefigured by the lawyer's courtroom attack. Even more importantly, however, the barrister's speech about mergers brings the whole film into a much sharper focus. It is this speech that allies the world of the gangs and the straight world of big business. It is this that allows Harry Flowers to function as a representative of all of contemporary London.

Despite these crucial differences, the first half of this shooting script is clearly closely related to the final version – much of the dialogue and scenes is identical. The second half of this version draws the arc of the intensified relationships that transform Chas, Turner, Pherber and Michelle in their Walpurgis night. But – and it is a very big but – Turner's house in Powis Square is a very different building in the shooting script. The isolated dark tower of the final film is, in the shooting script, an inner-city crash pad in which people come and go (including Turner to the police station after a drug bust). Nothing of this crucial part of the narrative remains. Even more astonishing, the final scene simply has Turner gazing from his bedroom window as Rosie and the boys drive off with Chas. The process by which the house in Powis Square is turned into a closed psychic space in which the inhabitants act out the drama of Eros and Thanatos has very little to do with the written text and everything to do with the actual shooting of the script.[1] Nevertheless I have used the shooting script wherever possible. It is written with real energy and style and even the clichés are revealing. There is also a great deal of explanatory scene setting and commenting on the characters' motives that I feel illuminates as well as limiting the meaning of the film, and I have included much of this material even though the finished work has a different narrative. I have added my own descriptions only where absolutely necessary, and they are set in a different font – e.g., on page 17:

Rosebloom stuffs the rag into the Chauffeur's mouth as far as possible. His cheeks bulge. The man whimpers. Chas walks round the car, his finger pressed lovingly on the Rolls's paintwork.

There is a fourth version of the script of which there is no trace in this edition. It is the release script of the version that Cammell and Roeg finished editing in London in the autumn of 1969. This is the version the Warner Brothers executives refused to release. They were shocked by the sex and violence, but they were even more horrified by the fact that the star that they had invested their

---

[1] For details of the shoot and also more information on the genesis of the script see Colin MacCabe, *Performance*, BFI, London, 1998.

money in, the convicted icon of the late sixties sex, drugs and rock'n'roll counter-culture, Mick Jagger himself, didn't appear on the screen until nearly an hour had elapsed. Warners were determined to re-edit: they wanted some of the sex and violence out, but above all they wanted to get their star closer to the front of the film.

He who controls the editing controls the film, and Warners quickly decided that the re-edit would take place in Los Angeles. This meant that Cammell had to travel with the film alone as Sandy Lieberson, the producer, had commitments in London and Roeg could no longer postpone the start of his next film, *Walkabout*, in Australia. The studio's plans to take control of the project foundered when Cammell encountered the editor, Frank Mazzola, who receives no credit on the film but who was crucial to the style of the first half. Together they were to implement a strategy agreed with the others that would get Jagger closer to the front of the film and cut down the number of minutes devoted to sex and violence while increasing the impact of what was left. Above all they opted for an elliptical, ragged style that cut against the rhythms of the narrative to produce an extraordinarily powerful opening. As an added bonus, much of the distinctiveness of the sound track, from the use of a synthesizer to the crucial 'Wake up Niggers' of the Last Poets, comes from this period in Los Angeles. The linear sequence of the original cut gave way to a montage of stories from a gangster's day, a vision of masculine hell in swinging London.

It is this repressed masculinity, this foundation of violence that is investigated and undone in the second half of the film as Turner, Pherber and Lucy use sex and drugs to play with Chas's identity and enable him to remake himself. It is Chas's liberation, the acceptance of his own bisexuality, that remains the film's astonishing achievement. The final scene between Chas and Lucy suddenly produces tenderness and love where in the opening scene Chas's only relation to his girlfriend was a bored, narcissistic politeness. The final film, however, adds an astonishing coda not found in any of the previous scripts. Chas, as his last act before leaving the house, shoots Turner and, as the film breaks all rules of coherent spatial construction, seems to merge with his 'demon brother'. The construction of this final segment of the film defies all definitive interpretation. It can as easily be read either as a moment of final liberation as each accepts the other's identity, or as a definitive repression as the forces unlocked by Chas's trip slam back into place.

The only text for this final sequence is the release script of the finished film and for both this and the opening sequence all the camera positions, which are as crucial to the meaning as the dialogue or the content of the image, are included in the script. In between, the usual conventions are followed and camera position is only mentioned when it is crucial to the narrative development of the film. The text is also lightly annotated so as to provide a certain number of contemporary references. The film is full of what Christopher Gibbs described to me as 'Donald's narcissistic injokes'. To take one example: the character Moody is played by John Bindon, who was famous all over criminal London for having torn off an opponent's ear in a fight and then presented his victim with the ear carefully tucked into a cigarette pack. Moody's first line is about an ear being torn off. I have not attempted to provide such full annotation, which would only be justified if *Performance* were to speak to new generations willing to buy a text two or three times this size. I have corrected the release script in a few errors of transcription. There are also, on occasions, half-lines that appear in the release script but are absent from the finished film. These differences may be the result of a final remix that Roeg demanded if his name was to stay on the film. All of these changes, as indeed ninety-nine per cent of the changes from the shooting script to the film, are improvements.

There are at least two different negatives. The first, presumably the American release and presumably not authorized by the directors, had Harry Flowers' voice redubbed and also does not contain the short black-and-white insert when Joey Maddox is shot. It also omits two very brief cuts to Turner in the scene where Joey beats Chas. The second, presumably the British release and presumably authorized by the directors, is vastly superior – *Performance* without Johnny Shannon's voice is not *Performance* at all. Unhappily, some of the video copies in Britain seem to have been struck from the American negative. I have not attempted to reconstitute *Performance*'s distribution history, so there may be other versions and the story may be more complex than I assume.

London, December 1999

# Performance

*The opening credits sequence begins with a shot of an aeroplane and then cuts to a black Rolls-Royce (which we will later discover belongs to the Lawyer) moving through the country before drawing up at a country pub, where the chauffeur begins to polish the car lovingly. The Rolls's progress is intercut with a couple (Chas and Dana) making love, which involves mirrors, whips and violence. The sequence is introduced by the Randy Newman song 'Gone Dead Train':*

> Shooting a supply from the demon's eye
> Instead of waiting for the time I hope I will
> Now the fire in the boiler up and quit before I came
> Ain't no empty cellar need a Gone Dead Train
> Yes a Gone Dead Train.

*The only front credits (in addition to the Warner Bros logo) are those of Mick Jagger, James Fox and Anita Pallenberg. The intercutting between car and couple is so fast that it is impossible to establish the exact relationship between the two. Indeed, particularly at the beginning of the sequence it is possible to imagine that the couple are inside the car. When the title of the film 'Performance' superimposes, we are watching Chas and Dana. Dana's head is between Chas's legs and Chas is watching her intently in a mirror that he holds so as to get a clear view. The camera pans left to right to hold on the mirror as the title appears.*[1]

INT. CHAS'S FLAT – DAY

*Tea maker alarm reading 2.45. Chas's hand enters left to turn it off. Chas performs isometric exercises in bedroom. Dana in bathroom applying make-up.*

DANA

Chas?

*Chas continues with exercises.*

---

[1] A shot by shot analysis of this extraordinarily complicated scene is provided in the Appendix.

Breakfast?

*Chas ignores Dana completely as she puts on her girdle.*

You're up.

> CHAS
> (*with total lack of interest*)

Yeah.

*Chas enters the bathroom and continues his self-absorbed preparation for the day, obviously irritated that Dana is interrupting his routine.*

You're going to be late for work, Dana.

> DANA
> (*from the kitchen*)

Cornflakes or Rice Krispies?

> CHAS

It's alright, I'll get my own.

> DANA

Confirmed bachelor, aren't you?
> (trying to gain approbation)

Fellah last night in the club said my voice was wasted on cabaret material.

> CHAS

Oh yeah.

*Cut to the black Rolls-Royce that we have seen in the credits sequence drawing into the Temple.*

> DANA

Shall I come over tonight?

> CHAS
> (*emptying ashtrays*)

I'll call you at the club about two. Half past.

*Even briefer cut to black Rolls in Law courts.*

*Chas has now escorted Dana to the door.*

DANA

Two?

CHAS

Two or half past.

*The Rolls stops and the door opens, we cut to Chas selecting a clean pair of underpants and cut again to him getting into a Rover*

Morning, Rosie.

*which drives away from the block of flats and into London rush-hour traffic.*

*Cut back to the Rolls. The Chauffeur holds the door open for the Lawyer, who walks up the steps past a sign which the camera holds on:* 'PARKING RESERVED for those having business in courts'.

*Cut to the Lawyer, and another barrister, preparing to enter the court. Cut.*

INT. ROVER

Travelling north, quite quick, Moody at the wheel, Rosebloom in front beside him, Chas in back.

Cut into very casual chat.

MOODY

It's eight o'clock in the evening, right? Kiddies are still viewing, aren't they?
(snarls at another car)
You bastard foreign female! . . . I mean, there's ketchup all over the screen, a bloke's got half his ear hanging off, ain't he?

ROSEBLOOM

Disgusting.

MOODY

I mean how are the kids going to grow up? It's not right, is it?

ROSEBLOOM

Definitely not.

MOODY

Where to, Chas?

CHAS

That car hire garage.

EXT. GARAGE

*The Rover enters the car hire garage.*

INT. GARAGE

*The Rover drives onto turntable.*

Close shot through car window.

A Spade looks casually, impassively, mildly curious at Rover. He turns back to his repetitive work.

ROSEBLOOM
(*to Moody*)

Put your tie on.

INT. CAR

Moody and Rosebloom silent in front, quite relaxed. Chas in back. Still. His face. His eyes look once round scene. He imperceptibly gathers his 'forces' (psychic). A tightening. Rosebloom turns gently to regard him. Pause.

INT. LAW COURTS

*The lawyer prepares to address the court.*

INT. CAR

*Chas starts to get out of car.*

INT. LAW COURTS

LAWYER

Gentlemen of the jury, I would solemnly suggest to you that what are really on trial here are the ethics of a community. Our national economy, even our national survival, devolves

6

upon the consolidation by merger of the smaller and weaker economic units with the larger and lustier pillars of our commercial culture.

*The Lawyer's speech is intercut with shots of the jury and of Chas, Moody and Rosebloom as they purposefully enter the garage offices. As he speaks, jarring electronic sounds begin to dominate the sound track.*

INT. GARAGE

Chas's face has assumed an expression of implacable fury.

Chas strides fast down the corridor, throws open the next door violently. On it is written 'Dispatching Office'.

INT. DISPATCHING OFFICE

About six women, two or three men, mostly seated at desks and a long switchboard/radio-table at one side.

The office is modern, well lit, well ordered in a standardized way; plenty of telephones, steel furniture etc., modern VHF radio equipment. A chatter of voices from the dispatches; the cab drivers' transmissions coming in over monitor speakers, etc.

Chas marches across the room. He is speaking with incredible fury and disgust to Rosebloom as he looks round the office.

> CHAS
> . . . What did I tell you? What did I tell you? Look at this pig-sty! It makes you sick . . .

The office is paralysed. *Chas sweeps files onto the floor. There are screams.*

*Chas rips paper from a typewriter, looks at it.*

> Correspondence . . . *not answered*!

A girl starts to rise from a typewriter. Rosebloom, not looking at her, places a hand on her shoulder, pushes her down into her chair, with the gentleness of a hydraulic press. *A man also rises and Chas sits him down with a terrifying Sssh. A hand rips out a plug from the switchboard.*

> I want that pig Pooley.

7

*Moody manhandles Pooley into Chas's presence.*

Are you Pooley?

POOLEY

Yes, I am.

CHAS

You know what you are, Pooley?

Chas advances. He speaks with growing, vengeful rage; evenly, not loud. The havoc he creates in the office is what makes the noise.

You're a disgrace. An *incompetent disgrace*. You're not fit to run a business.

*He sweeps papers, telephone off a desk.*

INT. LAW COURTS — DAY

LAWYER

. . . is business and progress is progress.

INT. OFFICE CAB DEPOT — DAY

Chas, confronting Pooley, very close to him; his voice a flat, maniacal monotone, trembling with suppressed fury. Moody behind Pooley. Pooley paralysed, now. Meanwhile, the girls at the switchboard, earphones over their ears, continuing to take and transmit calls to the car fleet, furtively and surreptitiously looking round to watch the 'row'. Chas, into Pooley's face:

CHAS

Where is your brother?

POOLEY

At the pictures.

CHAS

Answer yes or no!

*Cut to Rosebloom, soothing the spectators.*

ROSEBLOOM

Just about the office.

8

INT. LAW COURTS – DAY

> LAWYER
> (*addressing the jury*)

Stretch your mind.

*Low-angle shot of the jury, with ad lib chatter.*

INT. MINI CAB OFFICES – DAY

> CHAS

You need 'elp. 'Elp and protection. Well, we offered it, my guv'ner *personally* . . . you had an appointment. He waited fifteen minutes! You slag. *Fifteen minutes!*

> POOLEY
> (*despairingly*)

You said in the letter.

Chas's voice a low hiss – he looks about to explode like a bomb. Turns away, stares at radio equipment. The monitor speakers and girls still gabbling . . .

> CHAS
> (*runs finger along top of radio transmitter, holds it up*)
> You call this a service to the public? Look at this equipment.
> (*tears out some wires*)

*Not maintained* is it?
> (*to Moody*)

Now, you're a technician, Mr Wilson. Makes you weep, eh?

> MOODY
> (nods vigorously, saying)

Yeah, makes me weep.

He grasps the main radio transmitter firmly, tears it bodily from wall, looks at it carefully, and hurls it to the floor. *Pooley's shout of protest is drowned.*

It's obsolete.

INT. LAW COURTS – DAY

*This speech by the lawyer is intercut with images from the car hire firm and with increasingly surreal shots of the jury. The soundtrack is similarly invaded by electronic sounds.*

> LAWYER
>
> It is alleged by the prosecution, that the dividend of 15% which was declared on the non-voting B-shares was fraudulently designed to expedite this admittedly bold but in no way unethical merger – I say merger, gentlemen, not takeover – words still have meanings even in our days of the computer. The question is, was my client (*insert of newspaper photograph of Fraser*) a party to that fraud? Innuendo is a method I despise, therefore I say bluntly, that already you have heard sufficient to point to the responsibility and guilt of another party (*insert of low angle newspaper photograph of Harry Flowers*) – a guilty man, gentlemen, whose identity I shall not shrink from establishing in the course of my presentation of the case for the defence.

INT. OFFICE – DAY

*The final part of the lawyer's speech is delivered over images of an office. The camera moves through the space to focus on Harry Flowers sitting at his desk.*

> FLOWERS
> (*straight to camera*)
>
> Hello, Chas.

INT. MINICAB DEPOT OFFICE – DAY

*Chas places his forefinger very firmly on apex of Pooley's forehead.*

> CHAS
>
> You be there tomorrow. Number eleven Monk Street. Five-thirty, on the dot. Do you understand?

*Throughout this speech Chas has been stabbing Pooley's forehead with his finger. As he finishes, he removes Pooley's glasses. Pooley cowers and nods, a man destroyed. The electronic sounds cease.*

INT. OFFICE – DAY

                    HARRY FLOWERS
    Well, son. How was the clientele tonight?

                    CHAS
    Spot on, Harry. No aggravation.

*Very brief cut of Pooley cowering.*

                    HARRY FLOWERS
    What about this lawyer guy, did you get to see him?

INT. LAW COURTS – DAY

                    LAWYER
    That man (*shot of Flowers*), I submit should be standing where
    my unfortunate client (*shot of Fraser*) now stands.

INT. OFFICE – DAY

                    HARRY FLOWERS
    I can rely on that, eh?

                    CHAS
    It'll be straightened out in the morning, Harry. Don't worry.

                    HARRY FLOWERS
                    (*looking off*)
    He's a nutcase. Like all artists. But I can rely on him.

*Very brief shot of Pooley, eyes closed, destroyed.*

                    CHAS
    I know my . . .

INT. LAW COURTS – DAY

                    LAWYER
    . . . business is business and progress is progress. In the fluid
    state of business ethics pertaining today,

*The Lawyer glances behind at a clerk who guiltily closes the book he has
been writing in.*

11

we must protect the inalienable right of the smaller businessman to be conjoined in commercial union with an expansive—

*The Lawyer's speech has been intercut with ever more bizarre shots of the jury, who dissolve into an audience in a pornographic film at a club in Soho. Images of this pornographic film play over Chas's conversation with the Maltese proprietor. The electronic sounds return on the soundtrack to be replaced by the whirr of the projector.*

CHAS

You're worth it. Come on, Greasy.

MALTESE

Don't you understand?

CHAS

Pay me five thousand.

MALTESE

But this will finish . . .

CHAS

I haven't got any more time to waste.

MALTESE
(*overlapping*)

I haven't got to pay—

INT. OFFICE – DAY

MALTESE

Mr Molloy, you're bleeding me white, white as this wall.

CHAS

You're wasting my time.

MALTESE

Would you like a drink, huh? You like it with ice or with—

CHAS
(*shouting*)

You stink! You stinking foreign parasite.

*A Barmaid edges by.*

12

**BARMAID**

Excuse me.

**MALTESE**

Sssh. Please. My customers.

EXT. STREET – DAY

*Rosebloom sitting in the Rover reading. He is reading the Argentinian
writer Jorge Luis Borges' Labyrinths.[1]*

INT. CLUB – DAY

*Barmaid serves drinks.*

**MALTESE**
*(out of shot)*
Helga, please close the door.

INT. OFFICE – DAY

**CHAS**

You know, I don't think I'm going to let you stay in the film
business.

*Chas kicks him against the wall. The Maltese hands a wad of money to
Chas, who exits.*

**MALTESE**

British justice.

EXT. STREET OUTSIDE GARRICK (?) CLUB

Rolls-Royce stops bonnet to bonnet in front of Rover. As Chas
approaches the Rolls, its Chauffeur gets out. Moody, without appearing
to hurry, intercepts him as he (the Chauffeur) rounds the front of the
Rolls in order to reach and open the nearside passenger door. Moody
stands there, blocking the Chauffeur's way. The threat he embodies is

[1] Jorge Luis Borges (1899–1986) was an Argentinian writer who took part in the early
movements of European modernism after the First World War and then developed
his own very specific writing in Argentina. He was recognized outside his own
country in the early sixties and by 1968, the year that *Performance* was shot, no hip
room was complete without a translation of *Labyrinths*.

unmistakable. The Chauffeur stops. Opens his mouth – changes his mind, closes it. Then, rather bravely, he tries to step around Moody.

Moody steps in front of him again. This time, with easy precision, he leans his weight on his right foot on the Chauffeur's left instep. The man draws in his breath sharply.

> CHAUFFEUR
> (strangled, flat dignified voice)
> Here, what the . . . All right, let's keep our hair on, shall we?

Chas, completely disregarding the Chauffeur, briskly opens the door of the car.

> CHAS
>
> Mr Fraser?

> FRASER
>
> Yes.

*Chas helps Fraser out of the car, speaking slowly and softly.*

> CHAS
>
> I've got a message for you from an old pal. An old pal and an old partner. Who wants you to know, number one, that he's ever so upset about all this aggravation you've got and, number two, don't involve old pals, not even a little bit. Do you follow me, Mr Fraser?

*As Chas has been speaking the Lawyer has got out behind Fraser. Rosebloom has moved to the Lawyer's elbow.*

> LAWYER
>
> If you're an emissary from Mr Harold Flowers, it would be most improper for us to . . .

> ROSEBLOOM
> (*tapping the lawyer on the shoulder*)
> Sh, sh, sh, don't interrupt. And no subpoenas for old pals, old mate.

> CHAS
>
> And no snide insinuations in court, neither.

**LAWYER**

Now look here, I'm Mr Fraser's counsel and I warn you—

**CHAS**

And I know that, now shut your 'ole, Mr Counsel.

**LAWYER**

What did you say?

*Chas continues to talk to Fraser, as Rosebloom attends to the Lawyer.*

**CHAS**

Do you follow me, Fraser?

*Rosebloom points towards his mouth.*

**ROSEBLOOM**

'Ole.

**CHAS**

Now let's face it. They're going to convict you. But it's better to spend five years of your life in a nice comfy nick than the rest of your miserable existence in a filthy wheelchair.

**LAWYER**

Are you threatening my client?

**CHAS**

You bet I am, poncey.

**CHAS**
*(to Fraser)*

Do you follow me? Eh? Boy?

**FRASER**

Mmmm. I do.

**CHAS**

Good.

*As Chas turns to leave, the Lawyer attempts to accost him.*

**LAWYER**

Now listen to me, whatever your name is. I must insist that you address your remarks to me.

*Chas turns back and looks closely at the Lawyer for the first time.*

CHAS

Address my remarks. Okey-dokey, why not? Mr Butler, we've got his address, haven't we?

ROSEBLOOM

Why not, Mr Humphrey, if he insists.

*Chas remains looking at the Lawyer for some time; his lip is curled and his nostrils look as though he has just been assailed by an offensive smell. He breaks off for a parting word to Fraser.*

CHAS

Best of luck, Mr Fraser.

*The Lawyer shouts after the departing trio:*

LAWYER

You don't intimidate me nor my client.

*Fraser turns towards the club and hails a fellow member.*

FRASER

George!

GEORGE

Fraser!

EXT. MEWS – 7 A.M.

A mews composed of individual garages, flats above most of them. Early-morning activity. A newsboy doing his rounds. Birds singing. The sun is up.

The Lawyer's Chauffeur comes down the mews in grey uniform and matching peaked cap. He greets a bowler-hatted businessman setting out on his day. He opens garage doors (important-looking bunch of keys). The Chauffeur enters the dark garage. *Sounds of struggle. The light snaps on to reveal* the Chauffeur, purple-faced, supported by Moody's arm round his neck. Rosebloom takes an oily rag from a nail on the wall; primps the Chauffeur's cheeks, forcing the mouth open.

ROSEBLOOM

Morning, mate.

16

Rosebloom stuffs the rag into the Chauffeur's mouth as far as possible. His cheeks bulge. The man whimpers. Chas walks round the car, his finger pressed lovingly on the Rolls's paintwork.

CHAS

A tasty finish, a man of taste.

*He walks to the front of the Rolls where Moody is completing the tying and gagging of the Chauffeur.*

(*to Chauffeur*)

Looks after his property, your owner, does he?

*The Chauffeur's reply is inaudible through his gag.*

(*repeating the question*)

Does he?

*Chas continues round the car and places a bag on the bonnet of the Rolls-Royce. He takes out long rubber gauntlets, which he begins to put on. Moody, having secured the Chauffeur, moves round to help him.*

Regarding the car appraisingly; pulling on the gauntlets. Moody zips and buttons them for him. The camera cuts to a close shot of the 'Flying Lady' emblem on Rolls and then tilts up to reveal Chas pouring a jar of acid onto the bonnet of the car. He moves towards the Chauffeur. As he gets close to him, Rosebloom, who has been sitting in the front seat of the Rolls, sticks his head out of the door.

ROSEBLOOM

We've only got a gallon and a half.

*Chas hesitates, torn.*

CHAS

Better not waste it, eh?

(*to Chauffeur*)

Well, next time.

Chas commences the major work. He does the car from front to back, with geometrical precision. He is careful as he pours the acid. The acid, on the paint and metal. Colours. Fumes. Pretty patterns. The Chauffeur, watching destruction of the Rolls-Royce. The Chauffeur's face reflected in the paintwork of the car door. Acid runs down the

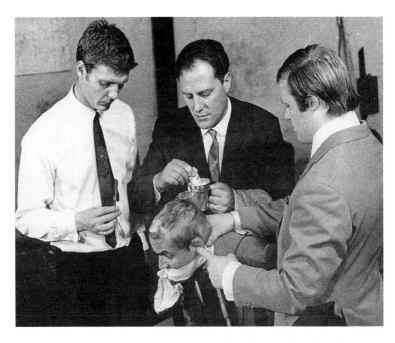

gleaming surface. His image dissolves. *On the soundtrack we hear for the first time what we will come to recognize as Turner's music.*

*The acid finished, the Chauffeur's hat is knocked off and while Moody holds him, Chas begins to cut his hair as Rosebloom makes a lather in a shaving cup.*

> MOODY
> (*restraining Chauffeur*)
> Hold up pal, you'll do yourself a mischief.

> ROSEBLOOM
> (*reflectively*)
>
> This takes me back.

> MOODY
> Your old man was a barber wasn't he, Rosie?

> ROSEBLOOM
>
> No. No, he wasn't.

> CHAS

Shut your 'ole, Moody.

> CHAS
> (*parody of a barber*)

No soap on the gentleman's collar!

> ROSEBLOOM
> (*to Chauffeur*)

Sorry, sir. It was an accident.

EXT. MEWS — MORNING ACTIVITY CONTINUES

*A Milkman makes his deliveries.*

INT. GARAGE

*Chas, cut-throat razor in hand, is now shaving the Chauffeur's head with the same intense concentration that accompanied the destruction of the car still smouldering in the background. Turner's music continues.*

> MOODY

Hair today, gone tomorrow.

> CHAS
> (*going instantly nuclear*)

I said shut your bloody hole.

> MOODY

He's a right lunatic, he is, eh?

The Chauffeur. His face. Tiny trickles of blood rivulet downwards from razor blade nicks unintentionally caused by bumps, pimples, etc. *Moody throws the remaining water in the small plastic bowl over him and throws the bowl away. He then picks up the bag and acid jar. They prepare to leave. Chas bends down to speak to the Chauffeur still gagged and tied to the front of the car. The car radio broadcasts a morning programme.*

> CHAS

Now I want you to mention what's happened here to your owner. Tell him I'll be in touch. Right?

Chas produces from his pocket a small steel mirror (back of manicure

19

set?) He holds mirror in front of Chauffeur's face. The man stares, looks away. Chas takes his chin firmly in one hand and directs his gaze to the mirror in the other.

                              CHAS

Trend-setting, sir, what?

INT. FLOWER'S OFFICE – NIGHT

*Flowers, Dennis and Gordon are discussing business. Chas and Rosebloom have just reported in.* Flowers in shirt sleeves and braces, sits behind desk. An air-conditioner hums. Papers, files, big ledgers, leather armchairs, photographs of boxers, a big safe. A vase of roses. *The scene opens with the camera on a painting of horse and rider.*

*Overlapping from previous scene.*

                            FLOWERS

I can rely on you. I can't say more than that, can I?

                              CHAS

                 (*combing his hair in the mirror*)

Thanks, Harry.

*Flash cut of Chauffeur bound to the destroyed Rolls-Royce.*

                            FLOWERS

Fourteen thousand quid we offer!

                            DENNIS

I call that equitable.

*Flowers (to Dennis) placing the painting, which he has picked up from the floor, in front of the mirror behind his desk:*

Three grand a week, that boy's grossing, or I'm a communist.

                              CHAS

Now what's all this about . . .

                            FLOWERS

                    (*interrupting*)

Now, Gordon, what we got in that file?

*Insert of Joey Maddox's betting shop.*

GORDON

Joey Maddox, licensed betting office 469, Fulham Road.
Acquisition of. Plus our letters, sir.

CHAS

Now what's all this about Joey Maddox? You steaming into
that slag?

FLOWERS
(*screwing up a piece of paper and throwing it into a
wastepaper basket*)
Course not. He's been invited to join our associated group of
companies, my son.

DENNIS

All he needs, Harry, is a little nudge.

CHAS

I'll nudge him for you. Don't worry about that, pal.

DENNIS

We've been courteous – courteous and generous.

FLOWERS
(*swinging round in his chair and regarding the boxing photos
behind his desk*)
He's an old friend of Chas's. Good pals they was. Like that
since they was kids. Game boy, eh, Chas? And a blinding left
hand.

*Insert of Joey Maddox throwing a left hook.*

CHAS

Bastard. As soon as he come into the poxy business. He . . .

FLOWERS

Now, now, calm down, Chas.

CHAS
(*rises to his feet – for the first time in the film he is out of control*)
Come on, Harry. You know I'm . . . He's a lying slag, he's a
grass and you know it and . . . I know it.

FLOWERS

Come on, son. Water under the bridge, that is.

CHAS

You know what I mean, Harry.

FLOWERS

All right. All right. Well tomorrow he learns what's true . . .
and what's not.

*Flowers takes painting down from his mantelpiece. Chas, who has risen
in his anger, begins to comb his hair in his reflection.*

Like small businesses in this day and age – is against nature.

CHAS
(*seated again*)

Lovely Harry, I'll learn him.

FLOWERS

No!
(*blowing his nose and pointing to emphasize his words*)
Rosie's gong to handle this spot of nonsense. I want that shop
redecorated tomorrow night. Get the Brown boys, they like a
laugh.

ROSEBLOOM

And Mad Cyril?

*Insert of rough-looking man about to throw a dustbin through the
betting-shop window.*

FLOWERS

Why not?

CHAS

What?

FLOWERS

Pop in – pop out.

ROSEBLOOM

Absolutely.

**FLOWERS**
You know what I mean . . . Be (*he snaps his fingers*) . . .

**ROSEBLOOM**
Placatory.

**FLOWERS**
Of course.

**CHAS**
Hold on, Harry.

**FLOWERS**
I like that, Gordon. Turn that up.

*Insert of Gordon turning up the volume on the muzak machine – this music has become more dominant as the scene has progressed.*

**DENNIS**
We want him to stay on and manage, don't we?

**FLOWERS**
Of course we do. His name stays over the door, if he wants. Right under ours.

CHAS

Let me see to the ponce, Harry. I'll decorate him and his shop.

Chas's frozen face and body – for an instant his abraded pride generates a phosphorescent threat. Flowers, relishing the instant, staring him down. As it passes, he leans forward. Words like axe-blows:

FLOWERS

Don't you ever listen to a word I say? Keep personal relations out of business.

A knock on the door. It opens – Moody's anaesthetic head pokes in, sees conference in progress.

MOODY

Oh, excuse me, but –

FLOWERS
(*loudly*)

Out!

Moody hurriedly withdraws.

Chas, your relations with Joey was double personal. Right? Right then! And what's my other thing I say? My motto.

*As Chas replies to this question colour begins to drain from the image and the muzak on the soundtrack begins to distort. We get close-ups of both Rosebloom and Dennis all colour drained.*

CHAS

At the death, who's left holding the sodding baby?

FLOWERS

Well, go on, what else?

CHAS

Harry Flowers.

FLOWERS

Right again. Me. Me! Me! Me!

*With each repetition of 'me' the sepia image of Flowers grows smaller and smaller until the final 'me', which brings the image back to colour and full size. Flowers moves to the window to raise the blind.*

All right, at ease, gentlemen. Anyone for a nightcap?

*We cut to the exterior and we see the blind rising to greet the dawn.*

INT. CHAS'S FLAT – DAY

Dressing. Deeply self-absorbed, precise. Expensive gear, uniformly styled in Hollywood Continental. Chas Devlin selecting cuff-links. He has a drawerful. *He enters the kitchen and turns out a light. Then into the bathroom.* Kneeling on the floor, he prises up a tile, takes two plastic-cloth bundles from a cavity underneath. He unwraps a very clean Smith and Wesson automatic pistol, cleaning gear, cartridge boxes. *There is an insert of the shaven Chauffeur tied to the Rolls.* He loads the gun briskly, tucks it into his waistband. He regards himself in the bathroom mirror. Smooths his hair, examines his hands. They're perfectly clean. He starts to wash them.

EXT. MADDOX'S SHOP – DAY

Plate-glass window and glass of door are smashed by dustbin thrown by Mad Cyril.

Window blind is rolled down. On it is written boldly:

Joey Maddox
Licensed Betting Office

(black letters on khaki blind).

INT. CHAS'S FLAT – DAY

He circles the room, obsessively tidying it (aligning ashtrays, magazines).

EXT. MADDOX'S SHOP – DAY

Smashed shopfront. A blanket has been tacked up behind the door to conceal the interior. A police car is parked outside; the driver in it. A couple of local ladies admiring the shopfront or trying to peer in past blanket over door.

INT. MADDOX'S SHOP

The interior of the shop is a shambles; covered with torn up ledgers, broken chairs, slashed upholstery (from benches), glass, confettied paper. Through a door (hanging from one hinge) behind the counter, the same scene is glimpsed in the small adjoining office.

Four people in the shop: Joey Maddox, confronting a Detective Sergeant, (Local CID), Maddox's chief factotum, Herbert (small, oldish, with hearing aid) behind him, echoing Maddox's indignation.

Clearing debris, a big thick-faced mate of his, Steve. Joey is strongly built (not tall) dark, good-looking; crude sensuality, sulkiness, good eyes, thick hair.

*The dialogue begins over the exterior.*

SERGEANT

We need a signed statement.

MADDOX

What for?

SERGEANT

Containing your allegations against Mr Flowers.

*Joey Maddox comes into vision, his hand pointing to the left of the camera.*

MADDOX

Allegations?

SERGEANT

Allegations.

*Steve's hand enters frame left proffering comb to Maddox.*

STEVE

Clean it.

*He gestures towards sergeant.*

Lots of filth around.

MADDOX

Yeah, cheers, Steve.
(*to Sergeant*)
Uh, listen . . . I'm not making actual allegations. I can't do that. What I mean, I got no proof, have I?

26

SERGEANT

Looks like you've got a war on your hands, Joey.

*Sergeant exits.*

Maddox, thunderous, kicks debris aside. *He seizes the lavatory bowl from the counter and throws it in the dustbin.*

MADDOX

I'd give a grand if I could get that ruddy Mister – Harry – Pervert – Flowers . . . right here . . . right now . . . I'd give a grand in readies.

*Joey walks back into the shop. Behind him comes Chas.*

Chas standing in the doorway.

CHAS

Will I do?

MADDOX

What . . . ?

CHAS
(*entering*)

I'd have rung up first, but your lines is always busy . . .
(*regarding strung-up phones*)
. . . all five of 'em.

Smartly, Chas takes Maddox's coat (flash Burberry) from coat-hook, steps to paralysed Maddox, rams it, bundled up, into his chest. Reflexively, Maddox clutches it.

CHAS

Let's go.

MADDOX

What d'you mean?

CHAS

Harry Flowers is waiting for you.

Chas walks out. His impenetrable back. Maddox follows him still holding his coat. Steve, suddenly aware, blurts to Maddox:

> STEVE

That geezer – that's the one, innit, eh, Joey?

He makes a move – half a step – towards Chas.

> MADDOX

You stay out of this.

*Shot – Rosebloom and Moody.*

*In car. Chas's white Jaguar approaches from opposite direction and passes them.* They look back over their shoulders, watching the Jaguar disappear. Moody betrays (rare) amazement.

> MOODY

Hold up. That was him that left with him.

## INT. HALL OF OFFICE – NIGHT

*Door with signboard reading:*
> SOUTH AFRICAN DEVELOPMENT LTD
> Presto Repossessions Ltd.
> SPORTSMEN'S MANAGEMENT ASSOC
> DAISY MAY TOY & SHOE FACTORS LTD

*Harry Flowers comes through the door followed by Joey Maddox, Dennis and Harrison. Flowers puts on hat.*

> FLOWERS
> (*out of shot*)

Look at this Vietnam strife!
> (*on*)

Down with red tape, eh? No taxman round here, my son.

## INT. NIGHTCLUB STAGE – NIGHT

*Stage with shimmering blue curtain. From behind it emerge Flowers, Maddox, Dennis and Harrison.*

> MADDOX
> (*out of shot*)

But Harry, I'm still a bit
> (*on*)

worried about my future.

28

Worried. That I will not allow, my son. Anyone worries you, you tell me about it. You're on the firm now, Joey. One of my own. United we stand, divided we're lumbered.

*Camera loses focus as they exit and then holds on black model in the background. Cut to close shot of photographer. Flash goes off, flaring picture.*

(*out of shot*)

Took over? No, Joey, the word is . . .

*Effects shot. Still of Flowers with his arm round Maddox*

(*out of shot*)

. . . merged.

## INT. THE HAYLOFT NIGHTCLUB – NIGHT

A bar, a few tables, ornamental ironwork, prints of flamenco dancers, diabolical photos of 50s show-biz 'personalities'. Quite well lit. Sub-muzak seeps (or a pianist). At the back beyond an open curtain, a card table, half a dozen punters plus kibitzers. Plenty of smoke and chat.

The clientele is mostly working class; dressed in proletarian boardroom gear – stamped with the indefinable dodgy-looking look of Performers. About three women at most. The taste of the place, the customers, is so bad it's interesting.

There is no atmosphere of furtiveness or violence. Cheerful racing chat, coarse banter – the odd toast: 'Be careful' . . . Only in the faces is the clue given.

A Home Office Crime Report describes it as '. . . an anti-social but non-demoralized society'.

The ambience definitely evokes an East End pub – clandestinely but solidly established on the first floor of a Mayfair house.

*Flowers with his arm round Maddox.*

### FLOWERS

You was merged, my son.

*Flowers picks up glass and proposes toast.*

To Old England!

*Close-up of photographer aiming camera at Camera. Flash goes off.*

*Flowers, Maddox, Harrison and Blonde Girl at bar.*

> (*to Harrison*)
> Jack, tell Chas to come over and have one with us, eh?

### HARRISON
(*exiting*)

Yeah, sure, Harry.

*Flowers turns to look at Blonde.*

*Effects shot. Pictures freezes and is over-exposed.*

*Flowers turns from Blonde to Maddox.*

### MADDOX

Harry, that . . . that shop.

### FLOWERS
(*overlapping*)

Exactly.

### MADDOX

No, listen, it's my whole life, Harry.

### FLOWERS

Exactly, Joey. Mine too. Mine too.

*Effects shot. Picture freezes and is over-exposed.*

*Chas advancing across nightclub. Camera panning with him and including Flowers, Maddox and Dennis as he stops before bar.*

> (*out of shot*)
> Speaking of which, Dennis, I'm not at all happy about the
> (*on screen*)
> tactless manner which Joey was brought here in.
> (*to Chas*)
> Chas, I told you not to bother Mr Maddox, didn't I?

CHAS
(*to barman*)

A whisky, please, Dave.

DAVE

Right away, Chas.

CHAS
(*to Flowers*)

Oh, was I tactless?

FLOWERS

Making him say that thing about his poor dead father. My
God!

CHAS
(*overlapping*)

Harry, let's have this little chat upstairs, shall we?

FLOWERS
(*crossing Chas and turning to speak directly to him
and into the camera*)

Who do you think you are? The Lone Ranger?

CHAS

I know who I am, Harry.

FLOWERS
(*out of shot*)

Course you do, son, you're Jack the Lad. I've known a few
performers in my time, but I tell you this – he's got the gift,
boy. Right, Denny?

DENNIS

He enjoys his work . . .

*Dennis pauses and picks up his drink.*

. . . and that's the half of it.

FLOWERS

D'you think he does, Denny?

CHAS

Oh, I do. I get a load of kicks out of it.

FLOWERS

Which can be a good thing, Chas.

CHAS
(*out of shot*)

Putting a little stick about.
(*on screen and looking at Maddox*)

Putting the frighteners on flash little twerps.

*During this speech Joey Maddox moves closer and closer to Harry
Flowers. When Flowers loses his temper Maddox is visibly delighted.*

FLOWERS

But it can also be a tricky thing. And I'll tell you why. 'Cause
you can get to enjoy your work too much, my son. And it can
slip your mind that
(*raises voice*)

you're bloody working for me, you berk. And when I say me,
I mean . . .
(*to Harrison*)

Tell him what I mean, Jack.

HARRISON

You mean . . . er . . . you, Harry.

FLOWERS

No!

DENNIS

The business!

FLOWERS

The business!

DENNIS

That's what he means.

FLOWERS

Correct first time, Den.

DENNIS
(*out of shot*)

In which you are a cog, boy.
(*on screen*)

A cog in an organ.

CHAS
You go to hell, Dennis, I know what I am.

DENNIS
(*out of shot*)
And it's the business of business
(*on screen*)
to push the buttons.

CHAS
And I'm alive and well . . . You push the buttons on that
(*close up on Maddox*)
thing.

FLOWERS
Right! We push 'em. Us! This terrific democratic
organization. Right, Joey?

MADDOX

Right, Harry.

FLOWERS

Same again all round, Dave.

DAVE

Right.

MADDOX

Let me do this one, Harry.

FLOWERS

The world's a dodgy place, my friends. I can't help that. But we've got progress. Look at the Yanks.

DENNIS

The new world!

FLOWERS

Organization! Listen, Chas . . .

*Flowers turns to find that Chas has gone. Flowers moves over to Dennis.*

FLOWERS

That boy's in bother.
                    (*pointing to his head*)
Up here.

DENNIS

He's an ignorant boy.
                    (*turns to camera*)
An out-of-date boy.

*Both Flowers and Dennis look directly into camera, nodding in agreement.*

EXT. SHEPHERDS BUSH. CHAS'S BLOCK OF FLATS (THE GRAMPIANS) – 4.30 A.M.

Chas's Jaguar draws up slowly, stops in forecourt. Without bothering to park it neatly, Chas gets out. He walks slowly, too steadily. Enters the building. *This sequence is interrupted by three quick cuts. The first two show red paint being splashed on a wall. We will soon realize that*

34

*this is happening inside Chas's flat. The third shot shows an anonymous arm spraying black paint on a red background. This is the first time that we see Turner and the house in Powis Square.*

INT. CHAS'S FLAT – 4.30 A.M.

Close-up of Chas's drunk face as he is punched hard. His flat has been methodically and completely wrecked. Smashed furniture, glass and crockery, television, records . . . Fragmented exultant gasps. *Maddox, Steve and O'Brien attack him.*

MADDOX
(*out of shot*)

Get him! Get him!

CHAS
(*out of shot*)

Let go!

*The sound of the fight is very loud. Chas tries to draw his gun but it is knocked onto the floor.*

STEVE
(*out of shot*)

Get it! Get it!

*In the tussle Chas damages Maddox with a kick to his left eye.*

Come on, Joey.

*More blows.*

You slag!

*In a short, inevitable time, Chas is finally down, semi-conscious, sprawled on the floor, very inelegantly. O'Brien gets a final kick into him.*

> MADDOX
> (*out of shot*)
> Hold his arm, now. That's it. Hold 'im.

*Maddox punches the pinioned Chas.*

Steve and O'Brien drag Chas into the bedroom. The room is in an (if possible) even worse state than the living room: the wardrobe doors open, showing his rows of suits – every one razor-slashed – the linings hanging down like silk ribbons. His shoes too are slashed; the cuff-links have gone into O'Brien's pocket.

Go on then! Come on!

> STEVE
> (*out of shot*)
> Come on, O'Brien. Give us a hand over here!

*Chas is on the bed. Maddox rips his shirt off. O'Brien pulls off his trousers. Maddox reaches across Chas's body on the bed and picks up dog's lead. Steve is brandishing a razor close to Chas's face.*

> (*in shot, panting with anticipation*)
> Shall I . . . Shall I decorate 'im? Eh, Joey?

> MADDOX
> (*backing away*)
> No, No, I'm not one of those.
> (*out of shot*)
> I'm not him.

*Maddox's final words are delivered over a crumpled photo of Chas in a boxing gym. Maddox approaches the bed and brings the lead down on Chas's back. Brief insert of Chas in bed with Dana.*

You love that, don't you? You little twerp.

*Steve lifts Chas's head up by the hair. Joey hits him with the lead.*

You vicious little twerp.

*Brief insert of girl's nails digging into Chas's back.*

Say it!

*Camera tilts up to word 'POOF' painted in red on the wall.*

*Maddox hits Chas again.*

(*out of shot*)

Say it!

*He hits him again with the lead.*

Say it!

*Maddox lashes him again. More inserts of Chas making love and stills from the gym.*

Go on . . . Say it!

*We dissolve from Chas's flat to Turner in Powis Square. Moroccan music and then dissolve back.*

(*in shot, softly almost desperately*)

Chas, say it.

*Chas, his head held by Steve, begins to speak.*

CHAS

I am . . .

MADDOX
(*exultantly*)

Yes.

*Chas's head suddenly hangs in Steve's hands; he's fainted.*

*Steve gazes at him in some alarm.*

STEVE

He's out, Joey.

MADDOX
(*panting from his exertions*)
Water, get some water.

*Steve goes to the bathroom while Maddox approaches Chas and looks into his face, holding him up by the hair.*

STEVE
(*from the bathroom*)
Why don't you give 'im the kiss of life, Joey?

MADDOX
(*in total fury*)
You shut your filthy mouth.

*Chas suddenly comes to, winks at Maddox and grabs him by the throat. O'Brien is dispatched with a kick of explosive violence and Chas cannons into Steve, who falls into the bath. Chas crawls along the floor. O'Brien grabs his leg. But it is too late. Chas has his hands on a gun hidden under the laundry basket. He rises like an avenging angel. O'Brien flees. Maddox inches, on the bed, away from the advancing Chas.*

Chas – look. Chas
(*out of shot*)
– you and me, Chas . . . we've . . . listen . . . look. Do you remember Mick? Remember. Chas. What's the . . . point . . . of . . . of . . . of this? You can't . . . do . . . that.

*As Chas aims his gun, the terrified Maddox raises the sheet on the bed in vain protection.* Chas advances inexorably, the gun held straight out in front of him, in his two bound hands, the end of the sheet trailing – trousers trailing – underpants sagging.

CHAS
I am a bullet.

*Chas shoots him. The bullet goes into his chest, knocking him backwards. The screen floods with red. He scrambles up.*

MADDOX
My God . . . My chest . . . it hurts . . . Look what you done! He – help me.

*There is a black-and-white insert of two boys struggling in a primary school playground.*

*Maddox is now at Chas's feet.*

> CHAS
> (flatly)
> You're dead, Joey. Do you understand?

*Maddox is dying. Very feebly, he sags onto his elbows.*

> MADDOX
> (*incoherently*)
> Yesterday and tomorrow.

*Maddox dies. Steve, terrified, dripping wet in bath sinks down. There is a brief insert of Turner's naked back. Chas struggles into his trousers. He glances without interest at Steve.*

> CHAS
> Get out of my flat.

*Steve lurches for the still open front door – trying to run. He gets out. Chas puts his head under the dripping shower.*

EXT. SHEPHERDS BUSH – DAWN

*The pre-dawn light. Steve running, stumbling, along a side street.*

INT. CHAS'S FLAT – DAWN

*Chas has opened up the hole in his bathroom wall and removes parcels and money, which he puts in a suitcase.*

EXT. SHEPHERDS BUSH – DAWN

*Steve running. A Copper hails him.*

> COPPER
> Hey, you! Just a minute.

INT. CHAS'S FLAT – DAWN

*Chas searches through the wreckage of his flat and finally finds an undamaged shirt.*

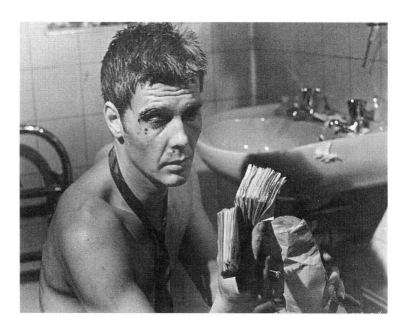

**EXT. SHEPHERDS BUSH – DAWN**

*Copper advances on Steve, who has his back against some railings.*

COPPER

Don't you bloody move.

**INT. CHAS'S FLAT – DAWN**

*Chas rifles through Maddox's clothes, extracting a pair of dark glasses. He gingerly puts a jacket over his bare and obviously extremely painful back. He ignores the ringing phone, turns off the electric fire, grabs a can of red paint and, taking one last careful look round the flat, leaves.*

**EXT. WANDSWORTH BRIDGE – DAWN**

Chas's Jaguar crosses the bridge, going south.

INT. HARRY FLOWERS' FLAT, REGENT'S PARK, FINCHLEY ROAD —
5 A.M.

His flat, in a big pre-war block, is large, most lush in a pretty
horrendous Finchley Road antique fashion. He has no pretentions to
Chas's 'contemporary' taste; he digs his sofas well tasselled and his
furniture good. A period nightmare.

Flowers in bed (a huge quilted affair). Propped up on his pillows,
wearing a florid dressing gown but no pyjamas, he looks dishevelled,
puffy-faced, pretty old. He is a deeply shocked man. He passes his
hands over the bed covers, his chest, his face. Moody is seated.
Harrison is walking up and down, talking in agitated fashion. Dennis
and Rosebloom enter.

> HARRISON
> Harry, I won't mince words, you're more than involved –
> you're incriminated. Look at the facts. The fact one—

> DENNIS
> (*interrupting and throwing his scarf on the bed and coat
> on Moody*)
> I'll tell you the facts. Business facts. Soon as they pick up
> Devlin, they'll be all over us, my friends. Press, taxman,
> copper, the lot. Do you know what they're going to call us . . .

*Rosebloom fiddles with light.*

> They will call us
> 
> (*out of shot*)
> 
> gangsters!

*Rosebloom continues to fiddle with light.*

> And it'll be goodbye to business.

> MOODY
> We'll be as popular as Hitler.

INT. A PHONE BOOTH, WANDSWORTH — 9 A.M.

*Chas on the phone.*

CHAS
I know you would, pal. I know.

INT. TONY FARRELL'S BEDROOM

A working-class flat.

Tony sitting up in bed. A young bloke. He's a commission agent (a dealer) at Covent Garden Market. His wife in the next bed. A baby. Tony, half asleep, looks shocked. He fumbles, talking in a low voice.

TONY
I just don't know anywhere, mate . . . Honestly . . .

BACK TO INT. FLOWERS'S FLAT

*Dennis and half-naked boy in bathroom.*

FLOWERS
(*out of shot*)

Where is he?

ROSEBLOOM
(*out of shot*)

We're looking, Harry.

*Dennis comes out of bathroom.*

DENNIS
Six figures a year, we're into. Six figures! And now this little bastard . . . He's put us in the stuck. Pity he exists.

INT. A PHONE BOOTH, WANDSWORTH

*Chas on phone. Jaguar in background.*

BACK TO INT. FLOWERS' FLAT

FLOWERS
(*sitting up in bed*)
I never sent him. It was me told him not to go. Don't get your personal relations mixed up in my business. I told him.

**DENNIS**

Told him?

(*laughs hollowly*)

That's a joke.

(*light is switched off*)

Like telling a mad dog who to bite, that is.

**MOODY**

I was bitten by a dog once. When I was a kid. It was a wire-haired terrier.

*Flowers is still lying in bad. Dennis turns light on.*

**HARRISON**
(*out of shot*)

Harry, I'm your legal adviser. You could be charged with conspiracy to murder.

*Phone rings.*

Hello?

**CHAS**
(*over telephone*)

Look, can I speak to Mr Flowers?

**HARRISON**
(*into telephone*)

Hello Chas?

*Brief insert of male model magazine that Moody is reading.*

**CHAS**
(*over telephone*)

Is Harry there?

**HARRISON**
(*into telephone*)

Yes, Chas, course he's here. Harry!

**FLOWERS**
(*out of shot*)

Eh?

43

> HARRISON

It's Chas.

> FLOWERS
> (*under bedclothes*)

Hello, Chas . . .

> (*listens*)

Are you hurt bad?

INT. PHONE BOX

> CHAS

Not too bad . . . You know already, eh?

> (*listens*)

It was just a . . . just an accident. Harry . . .

BACK TO FLOWERS

> CHAS
> (*over phone*)

I've got to get off the street.

> FLOWERS
> (*into phone*)

Yes, Chas. Yes. All right. We'll try to work something out.

*Flowers draws the covers over his head.*

INT. PHONE BOX

> CHAS
> (*into phone*)

Harry, you know I'd never lumber you. It's down to me this aggravation.

INT. FLOWERS'S FLAT

> CHAS
> (*over phone*)

But I've got to get in.

FLOWERS
(*into phone*)
Where are you? Humph. Chas, hold on a minute.

*Flowers emerges from the bedclothes.*

He's at Wandsworth Bridge Road.

DENNIS

Moody.

MOODY

What?

DENNIS

What would *you* do, Moody?

MOODY
(*out of shot*)

Eh?

DENNIS

With a mad dog, Moody? Where, the poor sick animal is liable to bite you.

MOODY

Bite me?

DENNIS
(*sighs*)

Without meaning to.

MOODY

I'd put him to sleep, Dennis.

Dennis nods. The fact has been verbalized; the decision taken by proxy. A perceptible feeling of relief in all quarters. Except Harry Flowers.

Chas's voice coming faintly from earpiece of phone.

INT. PHONE BOX

*We see Chas in the mirror of the phone box. He is doodling as he speaks. He draws the hanged man.*

CHAS
(*into phone*)
Harry? . . . hello . . . hello . . . hello . . . Harry?

*Chas crosses out his drawing and replaces the receiver. He leaves phone box.*

*Harry Flowers has now risen from his bed and is urging Moody and Rosebloom on their way.*

FLOWERS
(*claps Moody on shoulder*)
I don't need the details, my son. Off you go.
(*to all*)
I can rely on him . . . I can't say more, can I?

ROSEBLOOM
He's an artist, eh?

*Harry turns away and to the camera with a completely expressionless face.*

FLOWERS
My bath's running.

*As Flowers enters the bathroom and advances towards the camera his face takes on a sickly winning expression. He won't be bathing alone.*

EXT. STREET – MORNING

*Chas drives his Jaguar under a railway bridge. He takes the can of red paint from the boot and gets back in the car, where he mixes the paint and an emulsifier into a rough and ready hair-dye. As he applies a new colour to his hair, carefully observing the effects in the rear-view mirror, we cut back and forth to Turner spraying black paint onto a red wall in Powis Square.*

EXT. WANDSWORTH TOWN RAILWAY STATION – MORNING

*Chas in phone box.*

CHAS
(*out of shot*)
I can't explain now, Mum, but it's as bad as can be, now listen.

                    MRS DEVLIN
            (*out of shot, strong Irish accent*)
But Charlie—

INT. TELEPHONE BOX

                          CHAS
                     (*into phone*)
Now listen, Mum.

                          MRS DEVLIN
                     (*over phone*)
But where are you, Charlie?

                          CHAS
                     (*into phone*)
I must go away.

                          MRS DEVLIN
                     (*over phone*)
Oh . . .

                          CHAS
                     (*into phone*)
Now. Right away.

INT. MRS DEVLIN'S HOUSE – MORNING

                          CHAS
                     (*over phone*)
I might go to Aunt Mary.

                          MRS DEVLIN
                     (*into phone*)
Your Aunt Mary?

                          CHAS
                     (*over phone*)
Down in Devon.

                          MRS DEVLIN
                     (*into phone*)
Yes, go there. They won't look there. No. Not down in
Barnstaple.

INT. TELEPHONE BOX

> CHAS
> (*into phone*)

Right.

> MRS DEVLIN
> (*over phone*)

Now behave yourself, mind.

> CHAS
> (*into phone*)

Yeah.

> MRS DEVLIN
> (*over phone*)

And give her my love, won't you?

> CHAS
> (*into phone, overlapping*)

Okay. Thanks. Ta-ta, Mum.

> MRS DEVLIN
> (*over phone*)

Right you are.

*Chas replaces receiver and exits from box.*

INT. PADDINGTON STATION – 6.45 A.M.

Chas at the ticket office. He's not used to railway travel. He's paying for his ticket – 1st class.

> CHAS
> (*out of shot*)

I said Barnstaple, not Exeter.

> TICKET CLERK
> (*out of shot*)

I said change at Exeter, mate. Seven twenty-two. Platform four.

INT. TICKET BOOTH. CLERK SERVING CHAS

> TICKET CLERK

Gets in at ten past.

INT. BUFFET, PADDINGTON STATION – 7 A.M.

Chas seated at a table in the darkest part of the 'refreshment lounge'. He is reading a newspaper, head bent. As if willing himself invisible (despite his eloquent camel coat), he is now grey, shadowed, hunched. His shades gleam.

At the next table, a fat little woman is sitting, obviously waiting for someone. At her feet is a large box wrapped in brown paper; a carrying handle projects at top (it is an amplifier-loudspeaker).

*A waitress approaches in slow motion, bearing a cup of coffee and a sandwich.*

> WAITRESS

One and ten for the sandwich, love.

*The door of the buffet crashes open as Noel appears.* A black Pied Piper, dressed in tattered antique gear of motley colours, chains and beads, worn-down Indian boots, he carries a small bag and a guitar-case. His hair is a tempestuous growth of tiny coiled springs. At the next table, the small woman waves – prim, pleased. The musician strides over; shining smile.

> NOEL

Hello, Ma.

> MRS BONO

Noel.

Noel puts down his instrument case, wraps his arms round the woman, kisses her.

> NOEL
> (*overlapping*)

Thanks, Ma. You're a darling.

*Chas, paying attention to the conversation, looks around. His eyes fall on a young girl, but his attention is focused on Noel.* Noel speaks hipster-patois with a pure English working-class accent.

49

He said . . . You call that rock and roll? Well, I said, that's the sound, Mr Payne. That's what I'm selling you, man.

*(in shot)*

He said, My God, that's a black sound. Four times blacker than you.

Chas looking over the top of his paper, sideways. Incomprehension rather than disapproval. He returns to the racing news.

MRS BONO

Liverpool, tsk.

NOEL

*(out of shot)*

So I said, Cool it, cool it. It's a bad sound.

MRS BONO

*(out of shot)*

Aunt of mine comes from Liverpool.

NOEL

*(overlapping)*

I'll buy it, he says. You got a gig for six weeks.

MRS BONO

He's a shrewd one, is that. So Mr Turner's going to sublet your room then, is he?

*Chas is suddenly paying attention.*

NOEL

*(out of shot)*

Yeah, yeah, yeah, that's cool. I told him . . . I said, Turner, you are my landlord to which I owe forty-one pounds back rent, which I will send to you from Liverpool pretty soon.

*The camera begins a slow zoom past Noel towards Chas, focusing on Chas's ear.*

And he said, Yeah? So I said, Listen, listen, baby. All my things, all my gear, all my sounds, my big horn. Everything. My whole life stays right here at 81 Powis Square in this little basement room. He says, Okay, my son, go. I shall try to find a cool sub-tenant who has respect for another person's life.

MRS BONO
(*out of shot*)
That Turner. He's a drug addict.

NOEL
Ah, come on, Mum. He's just like—

MRS BONO
(*interrupting*)
He's peculiar. He's peculiar. He's a hermit. He can't face
reality. That what it is.

NOEL
Uhhh.

MRS BONO
A world of their own, these kids.

*The camera pulls back to reveal that Chas has left the buffet.*

EXT. PADDINGTON STATION – 7.IO A.M.

*The cab-rank in front of station. Chas getting in cab. To the driver:*

CHAS
Powis Square, Notting Hill Gate.

INT. HARRY FLOWERS' FLAT

*Flowers subsides in his bed.*

EXT. POWIS SQUARE

*Chas enters Powis Square. He is obviously in unfamiliar territory. Too
bohemian, not white enough. Glancing down on the doorstep, he notices
not only the expected milk bottles but Mars bars[1] and a trayful of
mushrooms. He rings the bell.*

[1] When Mick Jagger and Keith Richards were arrested for possession of drugs at
Richards' country house, Redlands, the papers were full of rumours of wild orgies.
In particular it was suggested that the Stones had been consuming a Mars bar
strategically placed in Marianne Faithfull's most private parts. This in-joke is the
only remnant in the finished film of the drug bust that was the central narrative
crux of the shooting script. For an account of what really happened at Redlands see
Marianne Faithfull, *Faithfull* (London: Penguin, 1996).

PHERBER
(*over entry-phone*)
This is a recording. Speak now. What do you want? (*huge raspberry*)

CHAS
(*into entry-phone*)
'Allo. Is Mr Turner there?

PHERBER
(*over entry-phone*)
Speak on the third beep. Beep, Beep, Beep.

CHAS
(*into entry-phone, overlapping*)
Oh, er, er, I'm a fr . . . I'm a friend of Noel's. An old friend. It's about the rooms.

PHERBER
(*over entry-phone*)
Ohhhhh.

CHAS
(*into entry-phone, overlapping*)
The basement room. I've just seen him off actually, me and his mum. Oh good morning, are you there? I'm a bit on the early side.

PHERBER
(*over entry-phone, overlapping*)
Hmmm, you've got the wrong house, mister. Fuck off.

CHAS
(*into entry-phone*)
No, listen. I've got it right here.

PHERBER
(*over entry-phone*)
Right where?

CHAS
(*into entry-phone, overlapping*)
The back rent. It's forty-one pound, right?

PHERBER
(*over entry-phone*)

Ummm – mmmmm.

CHAS
(*over entry-phone, overlapping*)

He said, Uh, uh, just settle up with Mr Turner and the room's yours, pal. Stroke o' luck, eh?

PHERBER
(*over entry-phone*)

Do you think so?

CHAS
(*into entry-phone, overlapping*)

I'm in the entertainment business. You know, uh, show business and, er, saw Noel at the railway. Hello. Hello.

PHERBER
(*over entry-phone*)

Oh yes, yes. Is that you?

CHAS
(*into entry-phone*)

Yes.

PHERBER
(*over entry-phone*)

The basement room – in the basement.

CHAS
(*into entry-phone*)

That's it, dear. That's it. Yeah.

PHERBER
(*over entry-phone*)

Down the back stairs.

CHAS
(*into entry-phone, overlapping*)

Yeah.

*The buzzer rings.*

PHERBER
(*over entry-phone*)

Push!

CHAS
(*into entry-phone*)

Do it again a bit longer.

*The buzzer rings again and Chas enters the house. We see him from Pherber's point of view on the first landing. His steps echo in this dark and mysterious house. He finally finds the basement stairs and begins his descent, footsteps echoing ever louder. He advances along the basement past a pay phone and finally notices Pherber in the lift. Pherber observes him closely, clad in little more than a fur coat.*

CHAS

Hello.

PHERBER

I didn't recognize your voice.

CHAS
(*out of shot*)

No?

PHERBER
(*out of shot*)

No.

CHAS
(*overlapping*)

Oh, no. I've been away, haven't I?

PHERBER

And I don't recognize your face.

CHAS
(*touching his bruises*)

My face? Oh, uh, you should see the motor.

PHERBER
(*out of shot*)

See the what?

CHAS

My motor. We had a little argument with a cement wall on the way up from Dover. Goodbye the Ferrari. It's down here, eh? First left I think he said.

*Chas opens a door.*

Oh, my mistake.

*Pherber comes out of the lift and follows Chas.*

PHERBER

Goodbye the Rolls-Royce. I know what you mean.

CHAS

Huh, look after my gear, pal. My big horn. Yeah.
(*out of shot*)
There I was, just back from the Continent, you know, from a Continental tour, and this had to happen.

INT. NOEL'S ROOM – 8.00 A.M.

CHAS

Oh, very nice!

*Pherber enters behind Chas and turns on the light.* Chas stands looking round Noel's room. He looks appalled. The room of a freaked-out spade musician, its walls papered with posters, bizarrely furnished, in great disorder; still full of Noel's gear and belongings (mostly records and magazines). To the eye of a hippy, charming. To Chas, a repellent muck-hole.

It's characteristic, eh? I'll take it. Uh huh. Dean's the name, Gerald Dean. Look, regards from Noel, I got forty-one pound for you. I owe it to him actually, but that's another story. I won't bore you with it. So a week in advance will be . . .

*Pherber reclines on the bed.*

PHERBER

Sixty-six pounds.

CHAS
(*slightly incredulous but writing figure in notebook*)
Sixty-six pounds?

PHERBER
(*unfazed*)
Plus one week deposit on the fittings and the fixtures, plus I should have a banker's reference.

CHAS
Listen uh . . . That's, uh . . .

PHERBER
(*out of shot*)
Extortionate.

CHAS
Uh . . .

PHERBER
Of course.

CHAS
(*calculating*)
Uh, well, uh . . . I'd say that was . . .

PHERBER
One hundred and thirty-two pounds.

CHAS
(*out of shot*)
Oh . . .

*Pherber is emphasizing the bareness of her legs as she plays with her fur coat. Chas is totally nonplussed.*

PHERBER
(*out of shot*)
How do you entertain?

CHAS
I juggle.

PHERBER
Juggle!

CHAS
(*out of shot*)

Juggle, juggle. I've a load of bookings here in London –
they're all A1 venues.

*Pause . . . then Chas holds up his hand, his smile is wan.*

No luck, have I?

PHERBER
(*out of shot*)

No.

*Pherber draws up her leg seductively.*

EXT. HOUSE – DAY

*Mrs Gibbs, the squat and lethargic housekeeper, and Lorraine, her
eight-year-old daughter clad in wellington boots, cross the road and
walk up the front steps. We are obviously in a West Indian
neighbourhood.*

LORRAINE

Oy, Mum, when's Christmas?

INT. BATHROOM – DAY

*Pherber takes off necklace and puts it with Chas's wad of five-pound
notes on the side of the bath. She picks up an 8mm camera and
approaches the mirror, where she shoots herself laughing and singing.*

PHERBER

People got the right answer
Because here we go.
One for the money, two for the show
People get ready because here we go.

*Pherber switches off camera and sighs.*

Goodbye the Ferrari.

(*laughs*)

INT. TURNER'S BEDROOM – 8.00 A.M.

*Pherber enters. She approaches the bed. She parts the curtains, steps up onto it. She takes off her belt and gazes down on the bed where Lucy and Turner are asleep. She lifts the camera and now we see first Turner and then Lucy through the lens. She turns off the camera and plays gently with Lucy's nipple. She turns on the camera and arranges Turner's hands so they protect his modesty as she films him full frontal. She begins in extreme close-up to kiss and lick Turner's nose and lips. As she takes off her dress, the two sleepers begin to wake to an erotic reveille shot in slightly overexposed 16mm.*

INT. NOEL'S ROOM

*Chas is lying on the bed. Lorraine is lighting a candle and singing.*

> LORRAINE
> (*out of shot*)
>
> Onward Christian Soldiers
> Marching as to war.
>
> You're pissed.

*Chas slowly lifts his head, looks at Lorraine and grunts. Lorraine laughs nervously.*

> (*in shot*)
> You've had one over the eight.

> CHAS
> No I haven't. I'm the new lodger.

> LORRAINE
> Do you want an aspirin? Wanna a cup of tea?

> CHAS
> Yeah, that'll be lovely.
> (*continues out of shot*)
> You got some turps?

> LORRAINE
> Turps?

> CHAS
> D'you want to earn a bob?

58

Two bob, mate.

*Chas groans to himself.*

CHAS

All right. Go and buy me a bottle of turpentine.

LORRAINE

Five bob, mate.

*Chas looks enraged.*

LORRAINE

Half a dollar.

CHAS

O.K.

INT. TURNER'S BATHROOM

Adjoining the bedroom, via a small passage. Hot water is gushing into the bath; old and capacious, marble-trimmed, set in the centre of the room. The environment and plumbing are, like so much of the house, of an ornate and ambitious conception; partly unfurnished, partly ruined. The room is large, and is, in fact, a combined robing-room–bathroom. Two long racks of amorphous raiment (a filing cabinet of antique duds) dominate one side of it. The water gushes into the bath. The sound of a lucid morning saga filters through the steam from the bedroom door. *Lucy and Turner, smoking a joint, are in the bath. Pherber is rolling joints at a table.*

LUCY
(*out of shot*)

So I say to this guy at the office, Why are you so mean? An' he just say, Your visa is finish.

TURNER
(*out of shot*)

Please!

LUCY
(*out of shot*)

And, an' you – you not in a place of learning, right?

TURNER

Right.

LUCY

An' you've got – an' you've got to get out of the British kingdom and go back to France.

TURNER

It's really insanity. You poor little thing. When was this?

LUCY

I don't know. Ah last week I think it was.

PHERBER

Last month.

LUCY

So I say, Pherber is teaching me English, you know, an' I guess the boyfriend is learning me his books an' everything, you know, and my magic stories.

*Lucy hits the water with her fist.*

TURNER

First thing in the bloody morning.

*Pherber lights joint, gets up, and discards her bathrobe.*

LUCY
(*out of shot*)
An' then 'e ask me, where are you living? So I say . . .

TURNER
(*out of shot interrupting*)
Hilton Hotel. I've got a crippled tap-dancer in my bloody basement.

*Pherber crosses the room and gets into the bath.*

LUCY

. . . I don't remember, and 'e say, Ho ho, this is very illegal.

TURNER

Yeah, said that.

So I say, It is a hotel.

TURNER
(*to Pherber*)
Listen, I don't want any more bums in my basement.

PHERBER
A juggler, madam.

TURNER
I don't want

TURNER and PHERBER
(*together*)
jugglers.

TURNER
I don't want him.

PHERBER
You'd love him.

TURNER
Yeah, you might like it.

PHERBER

You'd love him.

TURNER

Do you think I should wash my hair?

*Pherber smells his hair.*

PHERBER

Uh-huh. No.

LUCY
(*out of shot*)

Then 'e said,

(*on screen*)

You juvenile in moral danger . . .

TURNER
(*out of shot*)

Go on.

*Pherber sniggers.*

LUCY

An' you're not desirable.

*Pherber laughs and kisses Lucy.*

So I said, You stupid shit, an' I spit and I run away.

TURNER
(*out of shot*)

Well, just when I'd got my skull completely empty . . .

LUCY

Shower?

*Lucy picks up shampoo from side of the bath and the five-pound notes tumble into the water. There is a brief insert of Chas sitting in Noel's room with a huge picture of James Dean on the wall. Pherber begins to pick up the five-pound notes and plaster them on Turner's body.*

PHERBER
(*out of shot*)

Plus banker's deposit, plus money for fixtures and fittings . . .

LUCY
(*overlapping, out of shot*)
So I didn't get my visa.

PHERBER
(*out of shot*)
Plus references for one week . . .

LUCY
But I'm not worried.

PHERBER
Plus one week on account, that makes one hundred and sixty-seven pounds.

*Lucy has begun to wash her hair. Pherber gets up and reaches to help her.*

Here, give it me. I'll do it. I'll do it.

LUCY
(*out of shot*)
Oh, they'll never find me, anyhow.

PHERBER
(*out of shot, overlapping*)
There you are. Beautiful. I am not worried.

LUCY
Perhaps we shouldn't worry.

*Lorraine enters carrying a tray with mugs of tea on it.*

LORRAINE
Anybody wanna a cup of tea?

INT./EXT. OFFICE, COVENT GARDEN – DAY

Giant wholesale fruit, vegetable and flower market: trucks; noise; a lot of shouting and trading. The dealers are called 'commission agents'. Tony Farrell, Chas's friend, is a commission agent, whose office opens out onto the market. A colleague of his answers the telephone.

COLLEAGUE
Tony! Yer uncle for yer.

> TONY
> (*to workmate*)
> I should put 'em over there, mate.
> (*into telephone*)
> Oh, yeah.

*His face tightens.*

> Chas.

INT. BASEMENT – DAY

*Chas is talking on the payphone.*

> CHAS
> (*into telephone*)
> What's happening in the outside world?

> TONY
> (*over telephone*)
> Aintcha seen the papers yet, mate?

> CHAS
> (*into telephone*)
> No, I haven't bothered.

> TONY
> (*into telephone*)
> Well, they've really gone to town on you, my son. You *are* the front page.

> CHAS
> (*over telephone*)
> Oh yeah.
> (*into telephone*)
> What else?

> TONY
> (*over telephone*)
> Well, I've had the filth and I've had the firm. The law, they was nothing.
> (*gesture*)
> But your friend Rosebloom – he's funny, isn't he?

                    CHAS
               (*into telephone*)
No aggravation?

                    TONY
               (*over telephone*)
No, no.
               (*into telephone*)
But stand on me, uncle, it weren't your welfare he was on
about.

INT. TURNER'S BEDROOM

*Pherber is making up Turner for the day.*

                    PHERBER
Actually, he's obviously very very deeply involved with Noel.

                    TURNER
I don't want any invalid washed-up cabaret artistes in my
beautiful basement, sir.

INT. BASEMENT – DAY

*Chas on payphone.*

                    CHAS
               (*into telephone*)
Tony, I'm getting out. Out of the country.

                    TONY
               (*over telephone*)
Out of the country?

                    CHAS
               (*into telephone*)
Now listen, Tone. I'm going to tell you where I keep my
rainy-day money.

INT. BATHROOM – DAY

*Pherber, gazing at her back in front of the mirror, injects herself in the
upper thigh.*

TURNER

You shoot too much of that shit, Pherber.

PHERBER

Too much of Vitamin B12 has never hurt anybody.

EXT. COVENT GARDEN – DAY

TONY
(*into telephone*)

Behind the boiler you mean?

CHAS
(*into telephone*)

Well behind. Persevere. There's two grand in that bag. Tone. First off, I want you to nick a drink for yourself. Five hundred quid.

TONY
(*into telephone*)

You're a gentleman, Chas.

CHAS
(*into telephone*)

No, I want you to have it, Tone. You and Marge. Right, second off, I got to get a passport. There's a geezer – a' you got a pencil? Cypriot geezer, name of Thanopoulos.

*Lorraine comes from kitchen to door of basement stairway. She leans over banister, yells:*

LORRAINE

Hey, Johnnie, Mum says do you want an egg.

CHAS
(*into telephone*)

You got that, Tone. Good boy.

*Chas covers the telephone mouthpiece and looks up at Lorraine.*

LORRAINE

An' Turner says will you come up'n see him.

                    CHAS
All right, Lorrie. I'll be . . .
                (*into telephone*)
What a freakshow.

                    TONY
                (*into telephone*)
Where are you, then?

                    CHAS
            (*into telephone, vaguely*)
Oh, you know . . . on the left.

                    TONY
                (*into telephone*)
Oh. Yeah. Yeah . . .

                    CHAS
                (*into telephone*)
It's a right piss-hole, mate. Long hair, beatniks, druggers, free
love, foreigners . . . you name it.

*Tony laughs.*

But I'm not bothered, Tone. I'm well in and you couldn't
find a better little hidey-hole.

INT. LANDING AND STAIRS

*Lorraine leading Chas upstairs. She opens the door to the big room and
ushers Chas in.*

                  LORRAINE
In you go, Dad.

INT. BIG ROOM

*Chas enters.* The curtains are closed. There are a couple of lamps;
primarily a great filigreed Moroccan lamp that casts flickering light-
patterns over the scene. *Chas stares round the room. He is amazed.
The door closes behind him. He looks round. Lorraine has disappeared.
The curtains are shut. Chas lights a cigarette. He wanders around the*

*room and finally sits down at a desk. Over the whole of this scene we*
*hear the Last Poets.*[1]

> Night descends
> As the sun's light ends
> And black
> Comes back to blend again
> And with the death of the sun
> Night and blackness become one blackness
> Being you
> Peeping through the red the white and the blue
> Dreaming of boss black civilization that once
> Flourished and grew
> Hey! Wake up niggers or y'all through
> Drowning in the puddle of the white man's spit
> As you pause for some draws in the midst of
> Shit and you ain't got nothing to save your
> Funky ass with
> You cool fool!
> Sipping on a menthol cigarette around midnight
> Rapping about how the big apple is outta sight
> And you ain't never had a bite who are you
> Fooling? Me? You? Wake up niggers or you're
> All through and uptown two roaches are
> Drowning in each other's piss and downtown
> Interracial couples secretly kiss where
> Junkies are dreaming of total bliss
> Somewhere in the atmosphere far away from
> Here
> Beyond realms of white dimension guided by
> suppressed intentions as their cries! Cries!
> Cries!

---

[1] Little Willie Copaseely, a South African, declared this era to be the last age of
poets before the complete takeover of guns. On 16 May 1969, Malcolm X's
birthday, three converts to Islam, Jalal Mansur Nuriddin, Omar ben Hassan and
Abiodun Oyewole, adopted the name 'The Last Poets' for their performances,
which combined 'spiels' and music. Their debut album in 1970 reached the Top 10
album charts but also, singlehandedly, laid the groundwork for the emergence of
hip-hop and rap.

Go unrecognized except by their keeper the
Grim reaper.

*The music comes to an abrupt end. Chas looks up and sees Turner's image reflected in a mirror. Turner is wearing a dressing gown.*

> CHAS
> (*out of shot*)
>
> Good afternoon, Mr Turner.

> TURNER
>
> Good afternoon, Mr Ah – er.

*Turner switches on neon striplighting.*

There's been a mistake. You can't have the room.

> CHAS
> (*out of shot*)
>
> What?

> TURNER
>
> It's not for rent.

> CHAS
>
> Wait a minute. The lady's just said . . .

> TURNER
> (*drawing curtains*)
>
> 'The Lady said' – I don't tell her everything. My secretary. I've got a lot of work to do. I'm under a lot of pressure. Here.

*He hands the wad of fivers to Chas.*

> CHAS
>
> No, I don't want it.

*Chas drops cigarette ash on the carpet.*

> TURNER
> (*sees Chas's ash drop*)
>
> That carpet is two hundred years old.

> CHAS
>
> It looks it. A valuable antique is it?

TURNER
(*disappearing behind screen that divides the room*)
Listen, I gotta say goodbye now.

CHAS
(*out of shot*)
But the thing is, Mr Turner, I've got all my luggage
(*on screen, and speaking to the room divider behind which
Turner is now hidden*)
all my stage gear, it's all coming here from the Continent.

TURNER
(*out of shot*)
Your what?

CHAS
My luggage. My juggling, you know – stuff.

TURNER
(*peering round room divider*)
Why don't you go to a hotel?

CHAS
(*out of shot*)
Hotel? You must be
(*on screen*)
joking. Look I need a – I need a bohemian atmosphere.
(*Chas is addressing the room divider and the camera pulls
back to show Turner listening intently behind it*)
I'm an artist, Mr Turner, like yourself.

TURNER
(*emerging from behind the room divider*)
You . . . juggle.

CHAS
Why not?

TURNER
Why, why not? Why? Not – a jongleur? The third oldest
profession. You're a performer of natural magic.

*Turner has moved across the room and suddenly turns on music at very
high volume.*

*Chas startled – caught between two speakers.*

**TURNER**
*(picking up a microphone and performing a Mick Jagger jump to land right in front of Chas and shouting into the microphone as feedback builds unbearably)*

I bet you do. I can tell by your emanations you're an anti-gravity man. Amateur night at the Apollo.

*Vertical long shot of Turner moving clockwise, microphone in hand reflected in the ceiling mirror.*

Cheops[1] in his bloody pyramid. He dug a juggler or two, didn't he? Remember?

*Turner points up at the ceiling and Chas looks up. Cut to extreme close-up of a nipple. And back to Turner reflected in the mirror.*

And the tetrarchs of Sodom and Orbis Tertius. Am I right? Am I right, babe?

*Chas and Turner are now facing each other and as Chas replies, Turner lifts the microphone up to catch his final word.*

**CHAS**
More or less. Personally, I just . . . you know, perform.

---

[1] Cheops is the Greek name for Khufu, the second pharaoh of the 4th Egyptian dynasty (2575–2465 BC), who built the great pyramid at Ghiza. Juggling is depicted in the most ancient of Egyptian tomb paintings. The next reference: 'The tetrarchs of Sodom and Orbis Tertius' is simple nonsense. Tetrarchs (from the Greek for four) was a position invented by Philip II of Macedon in 342 BC when he divided Thessaly into four. It was not therefore used of Sodom, one of the 'kingdoms of the plain', which was destroyed in an earthquake some fifteen hundred years earlier. Orbis Tertius is a Latin phrase meaning a third of the world and is used by Borges in his story 'Tlon, Uqbar, Orbis Tertius', which is the opening story of *Labyrinths* and which deals with the attempt, over hundreds of years, to create an imaginary world that becomes real. The obvious explanation is that Turner is simply proving to himself that Chas is not who he says he is. This would go hand in hand with Turner's erroneous references to Rastelli, who is made juggler to a non-existent King of Tuscany and whose juggling record was ten not fourteen balls. It may be, however, that there is a sense to these references to be found in the world of magic, which is a much stronger theme in the shooting script and in Cammell's life than it is in the dialogue of the finished film. If there is a set of meaningful hermetic references, it has escaped this non-adept editor.

TURNER

Oh, you're a modest chap.
(*discarding the microphone and picking up some juggling balls*)
Because, after all, there was only one. Only one.

CHAS

Only one what?

TURNER
(*overlapping, and now seated and tossing the juggling balls in
the air*)
How right you are! Enrico Rastelli.

CHAS
(*overlapping*)
Please, you said it all, pal.

TURNER

Juggler to the king of Tuscany. Fourteen balls . . .

CHAS
(*overlapping*)
Now, about the room . . .

TURNER
(*out of shot*)
Fourteen balls!

CHAS

How about just on a . . . nightly basis?

TURNER

Right! On a knightly basis! On a horse! and blindfold.

TURNER
(*out of shot*)
Talk about a performer!
(*on screen*)
Of course, I'm not telling you anything you don't know, am I
old man?

*Turner stands up and throws one of the balls to Chas. He misses the ball
as it hits his chest and rolls into a corner.*

You can't stay here, old man.

*Turner throws the second ball gently to Chas. Chas makes no attempt to catch it.*

Not in the mood.

CHAS

Why don't you play us a tune, pal?

TURNER

I don't like music.

CHAS

Comical little geezer. You'll look funny when you're fifty.

*Turner has now walked past Chas and is sitting in a chair with his back to the performer.*

TURNER

You'll have to go. You wouldn't like it here.

CHAS
(*moving towards Turner with the wad of notes*)
Not *like* it? That charming little basement suite. I paid for it. I love it.

TURNER

No, you wouldn't fit in here.

CHAS
(*putting the money on the desk in front of Turner*)
I would. I'm determined to fit in. I've got to fit in, Mr Turner.

TURNER

I see. It's that bad is it, eh?

*Lucy enters the room in the background and observes the conversation as she disappears behind the room divider.*

I wonder, Mr Dean, if you were me
(*out of shot*)
what would you do?

CHAS

I don't know. Huh, it depends. It depends on who you are.
Which I don't know.

TURNER

Who I am? D'you know who you are?

*Chas has crossed the room and is looking at Lucy who is behind the room divider.*

(*out of shot*)

Eh?

CHAS

Yes.

*Lucy bends down to retrieve one of the balls.*

TURNER
(*out of shot*)

Well that simplifies matters. You can stay
(*on screen*)
on a daily basis. Yesterday till tomorrow? All right?

*Lucy leaves room watched by Chas.*

CHAS

Thanks.

*Pherber enters the greenhouse in the garden. She picks some mushrooms. The sun is shining. Chas observes her from Noel's bedroom. Lazy music. Chas turns away past a huge poster of James Dean and through beaded curtain into bathroom. He puts the turpentine on the shelf, takes his gun out of his waistband and carefully puts it in his jacket. As his bath runs he washes his hair in the sink. We cut to Pherber coming in from the garden before a series of shots juxtaposing psychedelic posters of Turner at the Albert Hall and Chas with red paint streaming down his face.*

INT. BATHROOM

Chas in his bath. Lorraine is sitting on the bathroom stool, studying Chas and eating baked beans.

CHAS
(*out of shot*)
He wasn't *that* big. I remember him quite well.

LORRAINE
He was an' all. He was world famous. When I was a nipper he was a chartbuster.

CHAS
(*lathering his face in the bath*)
They come and they go. Pop star! 'E 'ad a following. I never fancied his stuff myself.

LORRAINE
(*out of shot*)
I fancied him
(*on screen*)
old rubber-lips. 'E 'ad three number ones, two number twos and a number four.

CHAS
(*clearing his throat*)
Fetch that tea over 'ere, Lorrie.

*Lorrie carries the tea to Chas, who takes it. The rest of the conversation takes place with Lorraine at the end of the bath.*

(*out of shot*)
Didn't last though, did it? His success.

LORRAINE
Well, he retired, didn't he?

CHAS
Oh, did he? Well, what's he do now then?

LORRAINE
He stays, he stays here. He's writing a book and some music.

CHAS
Oh, is that why he's got a secretary?

LORRAINE
What?

76

That foreign bird – y'know, not the skinny one, the other one.

LORRAINE

Pherber.
> (*laughs*)

Pherber's his lover, mate. She co-'abits with him . . .
> (*out of shot*)

since years and years.
> (*on screen*)

Their love story's famous.

CHAS
> (*out of shot*)

Oh, yeah?

LORRAINE
> (*out of shot*)

Yeah! You don't know nothin', do you, DAD? . . . When's Noel coming back?

CHAS

Dunno.

INT. KITCHEN – DAY

*Lucy's turning the plug for her tape recorder over in her hands. Pherber shows her that she can't fit the plugs she wants together. 'Gone Dead Train' on soundtrack.*

PHERBER

That won't fit in, honey, look: it's all holes. That won't fit in.

LUCY

I know, I know how to do it. Come on. There it is.
> (*out of shot*)

Mmmmm.

*Lorraine enters the room carrying plate and Chas's empty tea cup.*

PHERBER
> (*out of shot*)

Look, this is the one. C'mon.

77

LUCY

(*out of shot*)

You're getting fat, Lorraine. Beans make you fat.

LORRAINE

I'm sick of beans.

LUCY

(*to Pherber*)

I don't really like that guy. I think he's horrible.

LUCY

(*out of shot*)

You don't really like him, do you? But what d'you want?

PHERBER

I don't want anything. I just let things happen.

LUCY

Why did Turner let him stay?

PHERBER

He changed his mind.

LUCY

Why? Why did he let him stay? Why?

INT. NOEL'S BATHROOM – DAY

*Chas is cleaning paint off his coat.*

MRS GIBBS

(*out of shot*)

Mr Dean?

CHAS

Mmm?

MRS GIBBS

(*out of shot*)

Would you like me to do your room now?

CHAS

Oh, hello, Mrs Gibbs. No thanks, dear, no. Tomorrow'll be
fine. Thanks a lot, love, thank you.

EXT. HOUSE – DUSK

*Downstairs window lighted.*

> TURNER
> (*reading, out of shot*)
> At this point something unforeseeable occurred. From a
> corner of the old room, the old ecstatic gaucho threw him a
> naked dagger, which landed at his feet.

INT. KITCHEN – DUSK

*Pherber and Lucy preparing mushrooms. Turner, with his back to them,
reading.*

> TURNER
> Dalmain bent over to pick it up. 'They would not have
> allowed such things to happen to me in the sanatorium,' he
> thought. And he felt two things. The first . . .¹

> PHERBER
> Yes. I know why.

> TURNER
> Yeah?

> PHERBER
> Yes.

> TURNER
> (*crying out in pain and holding his hand to his eye*)
> Ow!

*A fly lands on the table. The Borges volume flies into the corner of the
room.*

> LUCY
> (*out of shot*)
> What is it?

---

¹ This passage is from the end of the final story in Borges' *Fictions*. The story is
ambiguous as to whether Dalmain is really meeting a violent death or is simply
hallucinating in his hospital bed.

                    TURNER
                  (*out of shot*)
A

                  (*on screen*)
fly . . .

                    LUCY
A fly?

*The fly lying on its back on the table. Slowly its legs stop moving.*

                    TURNER
In my eye.

                    TURNER
Why?

                    PHERBER
            (*peeling a mushroom*)
Because you're afraid of him.

                    TURNER
                  (*out of shot*)
Yes.

                  (*on screen*)
Right. Right. And he's afraid too.

                    PHERBER
Of you.


INT. TOMMY GIBBON'S GYM, OLD KENT ROAD – 6.00 P.M.

A speed-ball being battered ferociously. Very loud sound. A young black boxer working on the speed-ball. *Tony Farrell is using a barbell.*

                    VOICE
Blower for you, Tony.

                    TONY
            (*over phone, out of shot*)
Hello, uncle. How are you?


                      80

CHAS
(*into telephone*)

Not bad, Tony.


TONY
(*into telephone*)

Now listen. Ah, I saw Thanapoulos. He said O.K. Yeah. He
can get you on a freighter. Direct to the big city. New York.
(*over phone, out of shot*)
'Ere, it'll cost you though. This includes seaman's papers . . .
(*into phone*)
. . . passport, graft to the skipper, all included . . .
(*over phone, out of shot*)
Nine hundred quid.


CHAS
(*into phone*)

Nine hundred? The old robber.


TONY
(*over phone, out of shot*)

Well, that's 'is rate.


CHAS
(*into phone*)

No, Tone, you done very well. You done very well. Good.
When do I go?


TONY
(*into phone*)

This week. Definitely. Yeah, no, listen. He wants a little
picture of you, mate yeah – a little photograph for your
passport.
(*over phone, out of shot*)
Y'know what I mean?


CHAS
(*into phone*)

Oh yeah, I get you. I get you.

**TONY**
(*into phone*)

Thanapoulos, he said, Now if your friend's smart, he'll wanna look decidedly different to what he normally does.

(*over phone*)

Grow a beard!

**CHAS**
(*into phone*)

Right, I'll think of something, Tony, don't worry.

**TONY**
(*over phone*)

Right then, I'll hear from you tonight.

(*into phone*)

. . . at my gaff, nine o'clock. All right? Chin up, uncle! The land of opportunity awaits eh?

*Chas replaces phone thoughtfully and opens a basement cupboard into which he glanced during the conversation. He sees a large number of empty picture frames. We cut to him on his bed cleaning his gun. The doorbell rings. He assembles his gun quickly and methodically.*

INT. BIG ROOM – EVENING

*The Myers twins[1] come in the front door carrying a painting. Shot of Chas sitting in basement. Close-up of portrait of Magritte.*

**TURNER**
(*out of shot*)

It's three years too late.

**TWIN**
(*out of shot*)

You said you wanted it.

**TURNER**

I can't afford it. I'm not sure if I like it, anyway. I'll keep the frame.

---

[1] The Myers twins were part of Salvador Dali's entourage. Although so dark as to look almost Oriental, they came from Brighton and earned their living by modelling.

INT. NOEL'S BEDROOM – NIGHT

*Chas throws the gun onto the bed.*

INT. HALL – NIGHT

*Lucy is showing the Myers twins out – they carry the picture without a frame.*

> LUCY
> Oh, come on, forget it. He never buys anything. It's all right to.

*Chas cautiously mounts the stairs and approaches the kitchen. Just as he is about to open the kitchen door there is a thud as a knife crashes against the door.*

INT. KITCHEN – NIGHT

*The knife rebounds from the door and sticks into the floor. Turner picks it up.*

> PHERBER
> (*out of shot*)
> Don't.

INT. HALL – NIGHT

*Chas opens the door to surprise both Pherber and Turner.*

> CHAS
> (*out of shot*)
> Oh, there you are.
> (*on screen*)
> Sorry to disturb, but has anyone got a sixpence for the phone? Ah can I – ah – use the blower up 'ere?

> TURNER
> (*mimicking him*)
> We haven't got a blower up 'ere.

> PHERBER
> (*reaching up to touch Chas's hair*)
> Ha! What in God's name has he done to his hair?

TURNER
(*out of shot*)

He's blown it.

CHAS

Yeah . . . well, that's it dear.
(*to Turner*)
I've got to ring up my agent again.

PHERBER
(*overlapping*)

Dyed.

TURNER

I fancied the red.

CHAS

No, no. It was the red was dyed.

TURNER
(*throwing knife back in drawer*)

Dead.

CHAS
(*out of shot*)

Dyed.
(*picking up eel which has just slithered out of fish tank on table and
returning it to the tank*)

Red.

PHERBER
(*out of shot*)

Dyed it . . . dead!

CHAS

Red . . . red!

TURNER

Van Gogh, eh?

CHAS

Oh, no, this is the normal.

TURNER

The normal?

CHAS

Yeah. I was just having a laugh. Having a laugh, you see, with my act, with my image. You know what I mean?

*As Turner speaks, the camera tracks to the back of Turner's head and then dissolves through it to medium close shot of Chas.*

TURNER

Yeah, I know exactly what you mean.

CHAS

Thought you would. Aah, 'e reckons, my agent, that – ah – time for a change.

*Turner's face is gradually superimposed on Chas's and then finally fades out.*

TURNER

It's time for a change.

CHAS

Well, I can see his point.

TURNER
(*out of shot*)

Yeah, so can I
(*on screen*)
personally, casting one's mind back . . .

CHAS

Yeah?

TURNER
(*out of shot*)

. . . I rather liked it.

CHAS

The, ah . . .

PHERBER

No, you fool, your act . . . your image. We've just remembered, see. We've seen it. We caught it in Hamburg. Your act.

85

CHAS

Oh yes?

TURNER
(*overlapping*)

Yes, it was fascinating.

CHAS
(*overlapping*)

Oh, mushrooms eh? I like them fried. Mm.

PHERBER
(*out of shot*)

Hungry, eh?

TURNER

Ha – even though – as one artist to another – it was a bit old-fashioned.

CHAS

Yeah, well . . . I am a bit old-fashioned.

PHERBER

Or was it Berlin?

*Pherber offers a joint to Chas.*

CHAS

No, thanks. Was it last year?
(*to Turner*)
Or was it sixty-seven?

PHERBER
(*out of shot*)

Sixty-six.

TURNER

Sixty-nine.

CHAS
(*out of shot*)

Was it Paris?

PHERBER

Goodbye the Bugatti.

                    TURNER
                *(out of shot)*

It was Wembley.

                    CHAS

Why not?

                    TURNER
                *(out of shot)*

No, Tokyo.
                *(on screen)*
Tokyo. That's right. The World's Fair.

                    PHERBER

Oh yes, it was Tokyo.

                    TURNER
            *(takes a puff on the joint)*

No, thanks.

                    CHAS

Yeah, it was Tokyo. Definitely. Speaking of which I just come
across downstairs on the floor . . .

*Chas takes photograph from his pocket and holds it out to Pherber and
Turner.*

    . . . This'll sound funny, but have you got one? A Polaroid?

                    PHERBER

Time for a change.

                    TURNER

Have we got one?

                    PHERBER

Yes, no.

                    TURNER
                *(to Chas)*

Yes, no.

INT. HALL – NIGHT

*Lift rises up into and out of frame. Pherber rides in it, holding tray.*

INT. STAIRS – NIGHT

*Chas and Turner mount stairs.*

> CHAS
>
> Just for a lark, I thought, eh? Little Lorraine set it off. Gave
> me the idea.

> TURNER
>
> Yeah, we often lark about with the Polaroid. Me and the girls.

> CHAS
>
> Oh-ah. I got a Leica N3 myself.

INT. BATHROOM – NIGHT

*Polaroid photograph cover being pulled off to reveal a picture of Chas in
a gangster outfit with a false moustache. Camera zooms back to reveal
Pherber holding the photograph with Chas sitting on the bed and Turner
lying by fireplace.*

> CHAS
> (*out of shot*)
>
> I never wear 'ats.

> TURNER
>
> Not even when performing?

> CHAS
>
> Never, no.

> TURNER
>
> Watcha wear then?

> PHERBER
> (*to Turner*)
>
> I'll show you later.

*As Pherber leans across to show Chas the photo she puts her arm round
his shoulders. Chas winces.*

> CHAS
>
> Aah well. Loose . . . aagh loose things.

PHERBER

Marvellous picture.

CHAS

Yeah, I never wear hats.

PHERBER

All right, you like the mushrooms fried. Sorry.

CHAS
(*overlapping*)

No. No. Aah.

PHERBER

Why don't you try this?

*Chas has a tray on his knees on which are the mushrooms that Pherber has picked and prepared. She feeds him.*

CHAS

I'll try anything once.

PHERBER

You'll like them, they're continental.

CHAS

Yeah, you're a good cook, Pherber.

TURNER
(*using lipstick pencil to outline his mouth*)

Are these . . . Are these photographs for narcissistic or publicity purposes.
(*out of shot*)
Uh 'cos if you're planning to disseminate
(*on screen*)
postcard size—

CHAS
(*interrupting*)

Have you got a drop of Scotch?

TURNER

No, sorry . . . offset litho reproductions of these by the thousand then . . .

CHAS

Oh, no, no. No. These are just for my agent.

TURNER
(*out of shot*)

You see my point?

*We see Chas and Pherber through the viewfinder of the Polaroid.*

*Pherber leaves Chas on bed and joins Turner behind the camera.*

CHAS

Course I can, course I can. Oh no, no, ah no, I'd – ah – I
don't want these to be seen by the general public. No.

*Turner takes photograph and activates flash.*

TURNER

Good. That's a load off my mind.

*Close-up of photograph. Two shots of Chas superimposed. Cut to all
three now standing. Pherber is behind rack of Oriental clothes. Turner
and Chas are standing by bath. Chas is handing Turner the
photograph.*

CHAS

That's a first class photo, Turner, technically speaking, but I
don't think it's a suitable image.

PHERBER

You don't.

CHAS

No.

PHERBER
(*walking round to sit on bath*)
I think it's perfect. Perfectly brown. It's you.

CHAS

Yeah, well that's it . . .

PHERBER
(*overlapping*)

It's both of you.

CHAS

. . . See, I don't – ah it looks – ah – a li'l dodgy, you know what I mean?

TURNER

I know what he means.

CHAS

You've – ah – you've gone too far.

*Chas exits shot leaving Pherber and Turner sitting on bath looking after him.*

TURNER

He means we haven't really got anywhere.

PHERBER

He means we've got to go much further out.

TURNER

We have to go much further, much further back, and faster.

PHERBER
(*crossing to Chas changing behind clothes rack and gently taking off his moustache*)
Wait a minute. Are you all right?

CHAS

Yeah. I'm fine, thank you. Look, what I've gotta have – is a little photo. I want a little black-and-white photo. Right?

*Chas starts to remove his shirt.*

B-but it's gotta be a little bit different. D'ya know what I mean? And black-and-white. Aaaaah!

*Chas is talking to Pherber. Turner appears behind him, from the other end of the clothes rack and sees Chas's marked back. Chas looks at him.*

It's nothing. It's the accident what done me up.

TURNER

You wanted a sort of passport size, eh?

INT. TURNER'S BATHROOM – 9.15 P.M.

Sound from record-player: a traditional blues. Chas lying on his stomach while Pherber sits astride him. He is stolidly enduring obvious pain as Pherber patches up his back. She is very cool; she shows only an objective enthusiasm in the nurse's craft. She is using the resources of a unique medicine chest. It is an antique receptacle of some beauty, and quite large. It contains an unrivalled collection of 80% used-up tubes of antibiotics, sun-creams, and theatrical make-up; baby lotions, hypodermic syringes, an unrivalled collection of pills, a foot-bandage, a Balinese opium pipe, Hong Kong aphrodisiacs, baby food, pornographic pictures, spare parts for a Japanese miniature hairdryer, and so forth.

> PHERBER
> (*overlapping*)
> It's interesting how things grow quickly – septic.

*Chas lowers his head and groans in pain.*

> (*out of shot*)
> I think . . . maybe we ought to call Dr Burroughs.[1]

*Turner crashes guitar chord.*

> PHERBER
> (*out of shot*)
>
> Give you a shot.

*Turner crashes guitar chord.*

> CHAS
>
> Shot . . . aaah?
> (*guitar chord*)
> No, No. You know what you're doing, Pherber.

*Turner starts playing guitar, out of shot.*

---

[1] One of the greatest writers of 20th century English and a leading figure of the American beat generation, William Burroughs was living in London in the mid-sixties. His cut-up technique, which attempted to produce meanings freed from the conscious control of the author, are an obvious influence on the editing techniques of *Performance*. Indeed Burroughs' most sustained experiment in film, *Towers Open Fire*, was produced in London. Amongst those who saw it was Nicolas Roeg.

                    **TURNER**
                    (*singing*)
You Better Come . . .

                    **CHAS**
                    (*overlapping*)
I've gotta get . . . I've got to get this little photo just right.

                    **TURNER**
                    (*singing, out of shot*)
. . . 'cos it's going . . .

                    **PHERBER**
What photo? Of who?

                    **CHAS**
Johnny Dean.

*Turner crashes guitar chords.*

                    **PHERBER**
                    (*to Turner*)
Baby, he doesn't know who he is.

                    **TURNER**
                    (*out of shot*)
He does.

*Turner starts playing guitar.*

                    (*singing*)
You better come in my kitchen,
'Cos it's going to be raining outdoors
With a woman I'm loving
Stole from my best friend
But the joker he got lucky
Stole her back again
You better come . . . in my kitchen.

He does.
                    (*out of shot*)
He knows. He's the bogey man.

CHAS

I'm alive and well. You push the buttons
(*out of shot*)
on that thing.

TURNER
(*singing*)
Woke up this mornin . . . somebody knockin' on my
door . . .
Woke up this mornin' . . . oooh . . . I said
Hello, Satan, I believe it's time to go.[1]

We push the buttons. He's the horror show.
(*out of shot*)
He's an old pro. He can take it.
(*on screen*)
He takes it, he dishes it out too. You can bet your sweet
fucking life he does. He's a mean bastard.

CHAS

I'm the Lone Ranger.

*Turner strums guitar.*

TURNER
(*singing*)
I'm gonna take you down . . .

*Turner plays guitar.*

(*singing*)
. . . by the riverside.
I might drown you . . . I might
Shootcha . . . just don't know . . .

[1] Turner is singing the Robert Johnson classics 'Come on in my kitchen' and 'Me and the Devil Blues'. Robert Johnson (1911–1938) is, for many, the greatest of blues singers and the most important influence on and inspiration for the popular music of the second half of the twentieth century. It is important to recognize that the soundtrack and geography of *Performance* (Notting Hill was the black area of London in 1968) enact the racial transformation of white society. It is interesting that Jean-Luc Godard was to try and use the Rolling Stones to preach a Maoist parable about the white appropriation of black music at almost exactly the same time in his film *One Plus One* aka *Sympathy for the Devil.*

'cos I'm mad with
ya . . . mad with ya . . . mad with ya . . .
Like Jesse James.

> *(out of shot)*
He's a striped beast. You enjoy your work eh? You've got the
gift.

INT. BATHROOM – NIGHT

> CHAS
What's wrong with the lights?

*Shot of the tray, with mushrooms, candles and goblet.*

> PHERBER
Yeah. Artificial energy,
> *(out of shot)*
it's pulsating into the voltage.

*Chas is lying on his chest with Pherber straddled on top of him. He is stoned now and his attention is caught by a candle. He rises, throwing her off him and the medicine box onto the floor.*

The flame. Hey, man, what is it?

*Chas in soft focus, holding his hand outstretched behind candle.*

> CHAS
> *(sighs)*
Yeah, yeah. I've never seen that sort before. They must be
scorching hot.

*Chas, now completely intoxicated, takes the tray off a mosaic table and begins to examine it.*

This is a . . . this is a very pretty table.

*Camera pans down to table. Pherber laughs.*

> *(out of shot)*
A very pretty table.
> *(on screen)*
I've an idea. I'd like to . . . How much do you want for this,
Turn?

95

*Dissolve to Turner and Pherber standing behind full-length mirror.*

(*out of shot*)
America is a blinding place for night life.

TURNER

He's on his way, that man.

*Turner spins the mirror 180 degrees to reveal Chas behind it and then spins it the full 360 so it reflects him and Pherber.*

How much did you give him?

PHERBER
(*holding up mushroom*)
Two thirds of the big one.

TURNER

That's insane. I can't make that scene.

*Exits.*

PHERBER

You should have thought of that before.
(*turns and calls to Chas*)
Johnny,
(*out of shot*)
Johnny? You feel better, huh?

CHAS
(*his back now properly bandaged*)
Yeah not bad, not bad. Pretty sharp.

*Pherber walks up to him. Chas taps his watch.*

Get a shift on.

PHERBER
(*out of sight*)

Sure.

CHAS

Where's Rosie, eh? We're going to nudge that slag. Don't you worry about that.

PHERBER

Johnny? Chas?

CHAS
(*out of shot*)

Yeah?

PHERBER
(*holding up mushroom*)

Look at this.

*Camera zooms in to extreme close-ups of mushroom.*

CHAS
(*out of shot*)

Cor! Horrible-looking thing.

PHERBER
(*out of shot*)

No, it's not. It's beautiful. You had one for dinner.

CHAS

Yeah?

PHERBER
(*out of shot*)

Uh-huh.

*Wide-angle shot of fireplace with mirror above and candles burning.*

CHAS
(*out of shot*)

You've poisoned me!

PHERBER
(*out of shot*)

Look, don't be crazy.

*Camera tilts down to mosaic table and then to bath with Turner, Pherber and Chas all standing round bath.*

CHAS
(*out of shot*)

You've poisoned me.

*Pherber walks up to Chas, handing him his gun.*

PHERBER

No-o.

TURNER

Oh, don't be ridiculous.

PHERBER
(*overlapping*)
No, no. We just want to speed things up.

CHAS
(*overlapping*)
You've got me drugged!

PHERBER

I want to get a shift on.

*Chas takes gun and falls over into bath. There is an overhead close-up Chas in bath screaming.*

*Cut to close-up of Chas listening.*

*Chas is seated on chair with Pherber cross-legged on bed. Turner standing throws mushroom onto bed and leans into Chas.*

TURNER
(*out of shot*)
I just want to go in there, Chas.
(*on screen*)
You see the blood of this vegetable is boring a hole. This second hole is penetrating the hole in your face. The skull of your bone. I just want to get right in there. Do you know what I mean?

*Pherber removes the bullets from the gun.*

TURNER
(*out of shot*)
And root around there like mandragora.

PHERBER
(*out of shot*)
Come on. You're beautiful.

PHERBER

We just dismantled you a little bit, that's all.

TURNER

Just to see how you function.

PHERBER
(*out of shot, and flipping bullets out of the magazine*)
We sat through your act. Now you're going to sit through ours.

TURNER

His act? They never get fed up with it, do they?

CHAS
(*out of shot*)

I'm a goer myself.

TURNER

Been on the road a million years. A million years people have been coming and dragging in to watch it.

CHAS

I like a bit of cavort. I don't send 'em solicitors' letters. I apply a bit of . . . pressure.

TURNER
(*to Pherber*)
He won't listen to me
(*to Chas*)
I know how you do it. I know a thing or two about performing, my boy. I tell you.

PHERBER

He had the gift too, once upon a time. You should have seen him ten years ago.

TURNER
(*out of shot*)
I'll tell you this.
(*on screen, transformed into a greasy rocker and the music
suddenly comes right up*)
The only performance that makes it, that really makes it, that

makes it all the way, is the one that achieves madness.[1] Right? Am I right?

*Pherber laughs.*

You with me?

> CHAS

I'm with you.

*Pherber on bed in wig with pieces of the gun in front of her.*

> PHERBER

He wants to know why your show is a bigger turn-on than his ever was.

> CHAS
> (*out of shot*)

How would I know?

> (*on screen*)

Well, I know a thing or two about the clientele. They're a bunch of liars and wrigglers. Put the frighteners on 'em. Give 'em a bit of stick. That's the way to make them jump. They love it.

> TURNER
> (*out of shot as Pherber takes off her wig and starts to fit it onto Chas*)

Boy's on a bummer.

*Dissolve to Pherber putting final touches to Chas the hippy in front of mirror.*

*Turner observes.*

> (*out of shot*)

Time for your new image.

> CHAS

Decidedly different.

> PHERBER

Now we're getting somewhere.

---

[1] Perhaps the single most famous line in the film is a clear reference to the French writer Antonin Artaud. An early surrealist and an actor in Abel Gance's films, Artaud sought in primitive ritual a means to transform bourgeois theatre. His writings were influential in theatrical experiments of the sixties.

**CHAS**

America's a blinding place.

**PHERBER**
(*whispering seductively in Chas's ear*)
Must you really go tomorrow?

**CHAS**

Tomorrow. Tomorrow he learns what's true and what's not.

**TURNER**

Nothing is true. Everything is permitted.

**CHAS**

Eh?

**TURNER**

The last words of the Old Man of the Mountain.

**PHERBER**

His motto. It's a thousand years old.

*Pherber is still adjusting Chas's clothes in the mirror.*

*The camera tracks in, losing Turner and Chas, to frame close-up of Pherber.*

Imagine yourself being a thousand years younger.

*Close-up of Pherber in mirror dissolves into close-up of Chas in mirror.*

*Chas crosses from one mirror to another to observe his new image. Turner is reading in the background. Pherber is still making finishing touches which gradually turn into kisses.*

TURNER
(*out of shot*)
'The old man was called, in the language of Persia, Hassan-i-Sabbah. And his people were called the Hashishin. He had caused a valley between two mountains to be enclosed
(*on screen*)
and turned it into a garden so large and beautiful that his people believed it was Paradise. And there was a fortress at the entrance, strong enough to resist all men. Now the old man caused those of his younger men whom he had chosen to be his Hashishin, his assassins, to be given a potion to cast them into a deep sleep, and to be carried into the garden so that when they awoke they believed they were in Paradise. And there were damsels and young girls there who dallied with them to their hearts' content so that they had what young men desire. Thus it was that when the old man decided to send one of his assassins upon a mission, such as to have a Prince slain, he would send for one of these youths and say, "Go thou and kill, and when thou re-
(*out of shot*)
turnest, my angels shall bear thee into Paradise. And shouldest thou die, nevertheless, I will send my angels to carry you back into Paradise." '[1]

They enjoyed their work.

*Cut to overhead medium close-up of Pherber lying on carpet naked.*

[1] This passage is from Marco Polo. A similar version is to be found in the *The Book of Grass: An Anthology of Indian Hemp*, edited by George Andrews and Susan Vinkenoog (London: Peter Owen, 1967) p. 24.

PHERBER

Are you in that garden?

CHAS
(*out of shot*)

Yeah.

PHERBER

Stay there. Never trust old men, old showmen,
(*out of shot*)
old wankers.

*Pherber is now on top of Chas on the bed pouring talcum powder onto his chest.*

I'm going to take you down to the riverside. I might powder you. I might polish you. I might make you shiny like a mirror. I just don't know. Hmm-hmm. What's that? What do you call it?

CHAS

Pectoral.

PHERBER
(*baring her chest*)
Do you like my physique?

CHAS

*(feeling her professionally)*

Yeah. It's in –

*(out of shot)*

It's in good condition.

*Pherber covering Chas's head with her dress.*

PHERBER

*(out of shot)*

I've got two angles. One male and one female. Just like a
triangle, see? Did you notice?

CHAS

Eh?

*Pherber reaches for small framed mirror and places it on Chas's chest.*

PHERBER

Did you never have a female feel?

*Chas lying on bed, arms outstretched, the mirror on his chest reflecting
Pherber's breast.*

CHAS

No, never. I feel like a man. A man all the time.

PHERBER

*(out of shot)*

That's awful. That's what's wrong with you.

*She moves the mirror from Chas's chest to his face so that we see a face
that is half Chas, half Pherber.*

*(in shot)*

Isn't it?

CHAS

What do you mean?

PHERBER

A man's man's world.

CHAS

There's nothing wrong with me. I'm normal.

*Pherber laughs and laughs.*

**PHERBER**
(*holding the mirror to her face so that we see Chas's face framed
by her hair*)
How do you think Turner feels like, huh?

**CHAS**
I dunno. He's weird. And you're weird. You're kinky.

**PHERBER**
He's a man. Male and female man. And he feels like me.

**CHAS**
(*overlapping*)
Hey, no, no he doesn't.

*As Pherber and Chas tussle on the bed the camera tracks past them to
reveal Turner in doorway.* (Note – The object of this scene is not
exposure of Pherber's bare skin, but rather the game that she and
Turner are playing with Chas, which is not primarily of a sexual nature
. . . In any case, several of the shots will be through the gauzy Indian
'mosquito-netting' curtains of the bed.)

*Throughout this scene Pherber is sexually teasing Chas.*

**PHERBER**
(*overlapping*)
Mmm.
(*chuckles*)
How do I feel? Huh? Tell me.
(*out of shot*)
Female feel!
(*she laughs*)
Hmmm. You love it. Come inside my square. I'll introduce
you to Eek,[1] the Light God. But be fast and change your
beautiful dress, or my curiosity will go elsewhere.
(*out of shot*)
Tell me, my Gluteous Maximus. Hmm? How does it feel like,
huh? Wha . . .

[1] I have been unable to find a reference to Eek in any encyclopedia of comparative
religion.

CHAS
(*out of shot*)
I said I'm not one of those.

PHERBER
(*overlapping*)
Big butch. Hmmm Rita Hayworth.

CHAS
(*overlapping*)
I said no. You're sick.

PHERBER
Ow!

CHAS
You, you, you de-
(*Pherber laughs*)
generate! You're perverted!

*Chas throws her off bed onto floor.*

PHERBER
Ah!

CHAS
(*out of shot*)
What's he want to get out of my face?

PHERBER
(*climbing back onto bed and kissing and licking Chas's leg*)
Mmmm. I'm going to polish you, mmm.

CHAS
(*out of shot*)
The 'ole. The 'ole. What's he want?

PHERBER
(*out of shot*)
May be a little mirror.
(*on screen*)
A little dark mirror.

CHAS

My mirror! No!

PHERBER
(*moans*)

A little dark mirror.

CHAS

He shan't. He shan't. The thieving slag.

PHERBER
(*out of shot, overlapping and with some desperation*)
Listen, listen! He won't take it away, you fool.
(*out of shot*)
He just wants to take a look at it. He's stuck! Stuck!

CHAS
(*out of shot*)

Why?

PHERBER
(*out of shot*)
Why? Because he's lost his demon, that's why.

CHAS
(*out of shot*)
Yeah?

*Pherber's next speech is over a particularly complicated sequence of shots. It opens with a shot of Turner sitting at synthesizer followed by a close-up of his face. There is a very brief cut to Chas falling onto the bed and then a cut back to Turner operating his synthesizer. The camera then tilts up to the ceiling mirror losing Turner to find his reflection. This dissolves (as Pherber talks of the stripy beast) to a tiny mirror held (in a prefiguration of Turner's death) against Chas's wig-covered head. The camera zooms out to reveal that it is Pherber who is holding the mirror. Chas turns to look at the mirror by the bed where Joey Maddox's dying face appears.*

PHERBER
(*out of shot*)
Yeah. He said he had it under control. Juggling all those balls. Millions of them. Until one day he was looking into his favourite mirror, admiring his image, see, and then suddenly he saw it a bit too clearly. And it was just a beautiful little freaky stripy beast, darling. So he thought maybe, maybe it's time for a change he thought.
(*out of shot*)
And then immediately, as he watched, the image faded. His demon had abandoned him. Puff! He was gone.

CHAS
(*overlapping and rising from the bed, his attention now firmly fixed on the vision of Joey Maddox that he has seen in the mirror*)
Yeah?

PHERBER
(*out of shot*)
He's still trying to figure out whether he wants it back. He's got to find it again. Right?

**CHAS**
(*overlapping*)
Listen, I've got to tell you something.

**PHERBER**
Go and tell Turner. He's waiting for you. He's been waiting a long, long time. You must be polite. Eh?

*Pherber throws him a shirt. Chas walks downstairs into the big room where Turner is busy at the keyboard while Lucy is dancing.* Turner looks very high; very good humoured, smiling to himself. He listens to the music. *Chas stands between the two speakers. Twice the camera pulls focus and explodes into clear frames. Chas begins to move with the music. He reaches out to Lucy and, missing her, sits down in a chair with a genuine smile transforming his features. He is simply beautiful.* Turner starts to do a small private dance; he moves in an odd, slow, ceremonial way; reminiscent of a ritual dance (which it is). (Is there a picture on the wall of Tantric dancers?) Turner dancing with Lucy. She is laughing as she dances. They are both very turned on. As she dances, Lucy covers a lot of space. *Turner carries a fluorescent striplight with which he accompanies the music. As the music builds we begin to see Turner as he must have been on stage. A first climax has Turner leaping and turning into the psychedelic poster that we have seen in the bathroom. Chas remains sitting and the music and light converge on his ear, which opens to reveal Turner in a suit and with his hair slicked back seated at Harry Flowers' desk. A voice says, 'Right again.' The following scene repeats many of the elements from pp. 20–25.*

**TURNER**
Me . . . Me! Do you call that equitable?

*Dennis, Rosebloom and Chas are also in the room. Dennis and Rosebloom are nodding along to the music.*

I like that . . . Turn it up.
(*singing*)
Didn't I see you down in San Antone
On a hot and dusty night?
You were eating eggs in Sammy's
When the black man there drew his knife
Ah! You drowned that Jew in Rampton

As he washed his sleeveless shirt
You know that Spanish-speaking gentleman
The one that we all called Kurt?

                    ROSEBLOOM

It was Mad Cyril.

                    TURNER
                  (*singing*)
Come now, gentlemen, I know there's some mistake
How forgetful I'm becoming
Now you've fixed your business straight.

                    DENNIS

We've been courteous.

*Turner singing to Chas who comes forward to sit in front of him. Turner keeps swinging the light so that it is shining on Chas's face.*

                    TURNER

I remember you in Hemlock Road in 1956
You were a faggy little leather boy
With a smaller piece of stick
You're a lashing smashing hunk of man
Your sweat shines sweet and strong
Your organ's working perfectly but there's a
Part that's not screwed on.

        (*rising and going towards Dennis and undoing his tie*)
Let's have a look, let's have a look.

*Moody knocks and peers round the door.*

                    MOODY

Excuse me, but . . .

                    TURNER

Come in, take 'em off. TAKE 'EM OFF!

*The firm begin to take their clothes off. Turner helps Dennis undress. Chas watches.*

                  (*singing*)
Weren't you at the Coke convention

Back in 1965
And you're the mis-bred greying executive
I've seen heavily advertised

Now you're the greygrey man whose daughter licks
Policeman's button clean
You're the man who squats behind the man
Who works the soft machine.

*The firm is almost naked and Turner has regained his rock-star look.
The naked Dennis and Rosebloom jiggle pathetically to the music as
Harry Flowers appears again behind his desk.*

Come now, gentlemen, your love is all I crave
You'll still be in the circus
When I'm laughing, laughing in my grave.

*Turner, as he disappears into the bathroom with a naked man, turns to
make a toast.*

Here's to old England!
                    (*singing out of shot*)

III

When the old men do the fighting and the young
Men all look on.

*Turner reappears from the bathroom with slicked-back hair and in
bankers' drag. He moves through the roomful of naked men, placing a
friendly hand on the clothed Chas's shoulder. He moves behind the desk
and as the song nears its end pulls out a drawerful of bullets that he
empties over the muscle magazines on the desk.*

And young girls eat their mothers' meat from
Tubes of Plasticon
Be wary, please, my gentle friends
Of all the skins you breed
They have a tasty habit
That eat the hands that bleed
So remember who you say you are
And keep your noses clean
Boys will be boys and play with toys
So be strong with your beast
Oh, Rosey, dear, don't you think it's queer
So stop me if you please
The baby's dead, my lady said
You gentlemen . . . why you all work for me.[1]

*Turner approaches the painting of the horse behind the desk, throws it
away and, raising his gun, smashes the mirror that is revealed behind it.
The final shot shows the three members of the firm sprawled completely
naked on the floor.[2]*

INT. POWIS SQUARE — NIGHT

*Turner is talking to a barely conscious Chas, still arrayed in his hippy
gear.*

TURNER
Go and tell your agent.

[1] 'Memo From Turner' is one of Jagger's most powerful songs, combining
electronic blues with surreal lyrics. Jagger, one of the greatest of lyricists, says that
much of the verbal surrealism came from Cammell – it is certain that the song
draws on the imagery of William Burroughs.
[2] In a film full of allusions to twentieth-century paintings, this shot is an obvious
imitation of Francis Bacon.

CHAS

Why? What time is it?

TURNER

You forgot to phone your agent.

CHAS

Er, ah I – I forgot.

TURNER

You forgot to phone him.

INT. BEDROOM – NIGHT

*Lucy and Pherber in the bedroom. Pherber is lighting a pipe.*

LUCY

These two freaks with shiny eyes like this – and a guy like this.
> (*out of shot*)

You've been giving him a hard time, haven't you. Did you
screw him?

*Pherber shakes her head. Lucy leans over and kisses her. Reaching up
Lucy picks up the gun.*

Hey, what is this?

PHERBER

Do you want it? It's yours – you can have it.

LUCY

Yeah? Is he a real gangster? Is he?

PHERBER
> (*chuckling*)

No.

LUCY

Mmmm.

PHERBER

Mmmm.

INT. BASEMENT – NIGHT

*Chas, minus wig but with bedraggled make-up and clothes, is on telephone. Turner holding coin to insert into telephone box.*

> CHAS
>
> You done me up. I forgot, didn't I?

> TURNER
>
> Mmm.

> CHAS
>
> He's got my . . . my passport. He's got my . . .

> TONY
> (*over phone*)
>
> Hello?

> CHAS
> (*into phone*)
>
> Tony? Hello?

*Turner pushes coin into slot.*

TURNER

Hang on.

CHAS
(*into phone*)

Who's that? Eh Tony? Huh! Hello, pal. Where you been?

INT. TONY FARRELL'S FLAT – NIGHT

*Marge lying in bed. Tony seated on bed.*

TONY
(*into phone*)

You forgot. Oh Christ Almighty!!

INT. TURNER'S HOUSE BASEMENT

CHAS
(*into phone*)

No, I had a bit of aggravation, Tony. It wasn't easy. Well, I've got the picture – I've got it right here.

TONY
(*over phone*)

Oh, that's great – that's great!
(*into phone*)

Er, look, that ship, it looks as if it's leaving tomorrow night. Yeah, somewhere . . . I just need the . . . the photo.

CHAS
(*into phone*)

Yeah, well, you got to – got to pick it up . . . Hang on – let me think.

TURNER

Eighty-one Powis Square, Notting Hill Gate. He can come here.

INT. TONY FARRELL'S FLAT – NIGHT

*Tony seated on bed, receiver to ear.*

CHAS
(*over phone*)
Eight-one Powis Square, Notting Hill Gate . . .

TONY
(*into phone*)
Eighty-one, Powis Square, Notting Hill Gate. Yes, Chas.

*The camera pulls back to reveal Rosebloom handing a cup of tea to Marge.*

ROSEBLOOM
You'll pick it up at nine-thirty.

TONY
I'll pick it up at nine-thirty.

*Moody is gazing at Marge.*

INT. TURNER'S HOUSE BASEMENT – NIGHT

CHAS
(*into phone*)
You all right, boy?

INT. TONY FARRELL'S FLAT – NIGHT

*Marge hands tea to Tony. Rosey, seated, observes.*

TONY
(*into phone*)
No, no, no I'm all right, Chas. I'm just feeling a bit tired, that's all.

INT. TURNER'S HOUSE BASEMENT – NIGHT

CHAS
(*into phone*)
All right, Tony – I owe you for this.

INT. TONY FARRELL'S FLAT — NIGHT

                        CHAS
                    (over phone)
I'm going to miss you, Tone.

                        TONY
Yeah, I'll miss you too, boy. Er, er, goodnight.

                        CHAS
                    (over phone)
Goodnight. I'll call you at nine.

                        TONY
                    (into phone)
God bless.

                        CHAS
                    (over phone)
Thanks, Tone.

*Tony lowers receiver out of the bottom of the frame.*

                    ROSEBLOOM
Thank you, Tony.
                    (as he replaces the receiver)
A wise head, eh, still on those young shoulders, eh?

*Rosebloom stands up.*

So he forgot did he? Forgot . . . but not forgiven. Eh, Moody?

*Moody is staring at Marge. She is beginning to stare back.*

                        MOODY
Pardon?

                    ROSEBLOOM
That's funny . . . wouldn't you say that it was unlike him,
Tony?
                    (out of shot)
It's unlike him to
                    (on screen)
forget an important thing.

*Rosebloom moves a picture leaning against the wall to gather his copy of Borges.*

INT. TURNER'S HOUSE – NIGHT

*Lucy is lying on the bed looking at slides of the pyramids. Pherber is asleep in the middle of the bed. Turner enters.*

> LUCY
> Why is he going to America?

*Turner gets into bed.*

> TURNER
> Why? I don't know. The place to go innit? For gangsters?

> LUCY
> I don't think so. He's going to get in some bad scenes again. He should go here. Look! Hmm?

*Lucy hands the view to Turner.*

> *(out of shot)*
> The mountains of Persia.

> TURNER
> *(out of shot, looking at the slides)*
> Yeah, maybe you're right.

> LUCY
> I'm sure there's some bandits over there.

> TURNER
> *(out of shot)*
> Mmmm.

> LUCY
> Don't you think?

> TURNER
> *(out of shot)*
> Could be.

*Turner climbs off the bed taking the gun with him.*

> Yeah, I'll tell him.

LUCY

I'll tell him.

*Turner rams home the magazine in the gun.*

TURNER

Tell me something. Do
(*out of shot*)
you think the mountains would be improved without the
bandits?

LUCY

Hmmmm. Je ne sais pas.

INT. BASEMENT FLAT – NIGHT

*Chas is asleep. Turner squats on the floor watching him.*

INT. TURNER'S BEDROOM – NIGHT

*Lucy looks at the sleeping Pherber.*

INT. BASEMENT FLAT – NIGHT

*Chas lying next to Turner groans into consciousness. His hand finds
Turner's body.*

CHAS

Oh my God! I feel like I've been through a cement mixer.

*Turner has been woken by Chas's hand and moves to kiss Chas. By the
time the kiss is finished, it is Lucy who is in bed with Chas.*

Chas and Lucy make love. The sun, dusty and narrow, enters through
a curtain's chink. He keeps smiling and kissing her face with a sort of
incredulous delight. He is gentle . . . he seems conscious of his
extreme good fortune in being entrusted with this rare person; then
. . . there comes a moment when we realize (the memory of a certain
caress . . . a gesture?) that without his being aware of it, Chas's
sensuality is an uncanny echo of Pherber's . . . when she was
caressing him . . . Lucy recognizes it . . . (does she say it?)

Something in Chas has changed. Perhaps, though, his screwed-up
ego would refuse to face the fact that for a little while anyway, he is

119

not trying to demonstrate that he is 'nothing but a man'. Perhaps he has realized that these three people are not concerned with the demonic and pathetic problems of gender that rot the human race . . . that they don't waste their lives and loves trying to define their sexes. Relieved of this duty he is marvellously at ease. Lucy is happy too. She says things to him in French. He understands perfectly.

LUCY

Tu es bien.

CHAS

French, are you?

LUCY

Yes, I'm French.

CHAS

You're a funny little frog. You've got small titties, eh?

LUCY

Yes.

CHAS
(*out of shot*)

Bit underdeveloped?

LUCY

Yes. What does that mean?

CHAS

You're very skinny. Like a little boy or something.

LUCY

Don't be ridiculous. Mmm.

EXT./INT. TURNER'S FLAT – DAY

*Pherber sprawled asleep on the bed. Turner walks from the window and climbs into bed.*

TURNER

Lousy morning.

INT. BASEMENT – DAY

*Lucy's hand holding amethyst.*

> LUCY
> (*out of shot*)
>
> This is for you. I found it.

> CHAS
>
> It's an amethyst.

> LUCY
>
> It's a purple amethyst.

> CHAS
>
> Yeah.

*Lucy removing ring from her finger puts it on Chas's.*

> LUCY
>
> You can have this too. This is a magic one.

> CHAS
> (*out of shot*)
>
> Oh is it? Thanks.

*Shot of jet plane over London.*

> LUCY
> (*out of shot*)
>
> Pherber's got a visa.

> CHAS
>
> They don't want to give you a visa?

> LUCY
>
> No.

> CHAS
>
> Why not?

> LUCY
>
> Uh, I don't know why not.

> CHAS
>
> 'Cause you're foreign.

*Lucy sighs.*

He likes foreign birds, that Turner.

> LUCY
> Maybe I come with you, why not?

*Another jet plane crosses the London sky.*

> (*out of shot*)
> But I don't want to go to America. I wish you'd be a bandit in Persia.

> CHAS
> What's your name?

> LUCY
> Lucy.

INT. BATHROOM – DAY

> CHAS
> (*out of shot*)
> He's got talent. He shouldn't have retired.
> (*on screen*)
> He should keep at it.

*Chas, looking in mirror, puts wig on.*

> LUCY
> (*out of shot*)
> He is stuck.

> CHAS
> Everyone knows who he is, still, don't they?

*Lucy in bath.*

> LUCY
> He likes you. Stay a little more.

> CHAS
> I can't. I, er, I've got to go along in a little while.

> LUCY
> I've got to go too. Maybe Pherber will come with me. For a

holiday in the mountains. Oh merde! Shampoo. It's upstairs
in the bathroom.

*Chas walks across room and kisses Lucy's wet hair.*

CHAS

I'll get it for you.

LUCY

Thanks.

INT. HALLWAY – DAY

*Chas enters through door and reacts to Rosebloom and three other
'chaps'. They are very polite, very discreet, the sawn-off shotguns barely
perceptible under the raincoats. One of them remains close to the window
of the ground-floor room, keeping an eye on the street.*

*Through door from hall:* Rosebloom speaks in his calm, considerate
way, like a doctor who has come to take away a madman,
accompanied by ambulance orderlies.

ROSEBLOOM

We got to be off, Chas. Harry's waiting for you.

CHAS

Yeah.

ROSEBLOOM

Some of the chaps 've come up to see you too . . . See how you are.

CHAS

Rosie, I've got to pop upstairs for a second.

ROSEBLOOM

No, we've not got time . . . We've got to get down to the country.

CHAS

We've got time. We've got a minute. Else you'll have to give it to me right here. Right here.

*Chas points at his stomach and the gun tucked into his trousers.*

(*out of shot*)

Won't you, Rosie?

ROSEBLOOM

All right . . . Make it two minutes. You'll let me have the shooter as soon as you come down, right?

CHAS

Right.

*Chas exits up the stairs.*

ROSEBLOOM

(*after him*)

There's a couple of chaps on the roof, Chas, and a couple in the garden.

INT. TURNER'S BEDROOM – DAY

*Chas enters. Turner sits up in bed. Pherber is asleep beside him.*

CHAS

I've got to be off now.

TURNER

No, I'm going to talk to you some more.

CHAS

No, I've got to shoot off now.

TURNER
(*out of shot*)

I might come with you then.

*Chas walks around the bed, carefully picking up a robe.*

CHAS
(*through the rope curtains around the bed*)

Humph, you don't know where I'm going, pal.

TURNER
(*with Pherber now awake beside him*)

I do.

*As the music builds, Chas walks to the window to check that the house is as surrounded as Rosebloom has claimed. It is.*

I don't know.

*Turner sinks his head down onto his chest. Chas raises his gun making sure that the magazine is rammed home.*

CHAS

Yeah, you do.

*Pherber rises up in the bed, holding her hand out, yelling.*

PHERBER
(*as Chas fires into Turner's head*)

NO!

*High-angle close-up of top of Turner's head. Bullet enters it. Camera zooms in to extreme close-up of wound as it opens up. Shot changes to camera moving down wound as it opens up. In the wound the image of Borges appears and the camera breaks through the image, which shatters as a glass mirror while a heavenly choir cuts in on the soundtrack. The camera has now broken through to the exterior of the house. The camera tilts down.*

EXT. STREET – DAY

*Long shot, Chas and Rosebloom emerging right from house, walking left down steps. Medium-long shot, Chas and Mad Cyril walking along street. Hand-held camera moving in with them.*

INT. TURNER'S HOUSE – DAY

*High-angle medium-close shot, Rosebloom opening door to reveal shot of Turner's bedroom. He turns, half-closing door behind him.*

EXT. POWIS SQUARE – DAY

*Hand-held camera moving in with medium-long shot of Chas and Mad Cyril as they walk.*

INT. BASEMENT TURNER'S HOUSE – DAY

*Long shot basement flat. Rosebloom enters through door holding note. He throws it onto bed.*

LUCY
(*out of shot, water splashing*)

Chas? Chas!

*High-angle close-up of note reading: 'GONE TO PERSIA X CHAS.'*

INT. CORRIDOR – DAY

*Long shot Rosebloom closes basement flat door. Close shot of Pherber blood spattered over her neck and shirt. Long shot of Rosebloom walking down corridor. Pherber's arm enters shot. High-angle medium-close shot of Pherber pulling door shut and hiding herself. Long shot of Rosebloom walking through basement. He stops in medium-long shot by cupboard door. High-angle medium-close shot of Rosebloom's hand opening door to reveal Turner seated in cupboard, amongst empty picture frames, dead. Rosebloom's hand closes door, obscuring Turner.*

EXT. POWIS SQUARE – DAY

*Hand-held camera moving with Chas and Mad Cyril in medium-long shot. Medium shot, chap leaning against wall. Hand-held camera*

*panning slightly left to right then moving in past him, then panning to
reveal in long shot a child walking, and behind, in very long shot,
Harry Flowers' white Rolls-Royce.*

INT. TURNER'S HOUSE – DAY

*High-angle medium-close shot door. Rosebloom enters right in medium-
close shot and stands back to camera.*

INT. ROOM – DAY

*Rosebloom pushes door and peers round it. High-angle medium shot of
camera tracking in and panning left to right around objects in the
room.*

*Dissolves to:*

*Medium-long shot camera tracking in past bay tree to reveal couch
covered with cushions. Low level medium shot furniture. Light is
switched off and Rosebloom appears from right in medium shot and exits
through doorway.*

EXT. POWIS SQUARE – DAY

*Long shot white Rolls-Royce. Hand-held camera moving towards it.
Chap walks forward and opens door revealing Harry Flowers in
medium-long shot seated in the back of the car.*

FLOWERS

Hello, Chas.

*Medium-long shot, Chas climbing into white Rolls-Royce. Chap holds
door open as camera pans left to right, losing chap as he closes door,
revealing Harry Flowers seated right back to Camera.*

*Long shot of white Rolls-Royce driving. Camera zooms in and pans
right to left holding in medium-close shot Turner looking out through
window. Camera then zooms out and holds as white Rolls-Royce drives
out of shot.*

EXT. COUNTRYSIDE – DAY

*Camera panning right to left with medium-close/long shot of white*

*Rolls-Royce as it exits over brow of the hill. Camera starts to zoom in as car reappears in very long shot.*[1]

SUPERIMPOSED TITLE ROLLS IN BOTTOM FRAME:

| | |
|---|---|
| JAMES FOX | CHAS |
| MICK JAGGER | TURNER |
| ANITA PALLENBERG | PHERBER |
| MICHELE BRETON | LUCY |
| ANN SIDNEY | DANA |
| JOHN BINDON | MOODY |
| STANLEY MEADOWS | ROSEBLOOM |
| ALLAN CUTHBERTSON | THE LAWYER |
| ANTONY MORTON | DENNIS |
| JOHNNY SHANNON | HARRY FLOWERS |
| ANTHONY VALENTINE | JOEY MADDOCKS |
| KEN COLLEY | TONY FARRELL |
| JOHN STERLAND | THE CHAUFFEUR |
| LLARAINE WICKENS | LORRAINE |

*As the cast credits finish the heavenly choir cuts out and Randy Newman comes in. 'Gone Dead Train' continues right until the end of the credits.*

Waitin' at the station with a heavy loaded sack
Saving up and holding just to spill
Shootin' a supply from my demon's eye
Instead of waitin' for the time I hope I will
The fire in my boiler up and quit before I came
And there ain't no empty cellar need a gone dead train
Yes, a gone dead train
You've got to teach it to earn
You know it's a gone dead train
You got to teach it to burn
Well, there ain't no easy way when your daily runs a downhill
pull
Wishing for some jelly roll wool

---

[1] Right before the end of the editing period in England, Roeg had the idea that the final shot of the film would show the white Rolls-Royce pulling out of Fifth Avenue and turning into Central Park. Cammell's enthusiastic pleas for additional money for this final shot fell on deaf ears.

Ain't no switch been made
With a juicy lemon find
A spring to run a dry well full
The fire in my boiler up and quit before I came
Ain't no empty cellar need gone.

*Camera holds as the white Rolls-Royce disappears over the brow of another hill.*

*Superimposed title rolls out top frame and superimposed title jumps in:*
written by
DONALD CAMMELL
photography by
NICOLAS ROEG, B.S.C.
produced by
SANFORD LIEBERSON

*Freeze frame of Victorian slide of Persian mountains and desert.*

directed by
DONALD CAMMELL and NICOLAS ROEG

INT. TURNER'S FLAT – DAY

*High-angle medium shot of Borges's book and cover lying on the floor.*

music by Jack Nitzche
Turner's song
MEMO FROM T
written by MICK JAGGER

*Dissolve to high-angle close shot of patchwork quilt.*

Music conducted by RANDY NEWMAN

Played by RY COODER    MILT HOLLAND
BOBBY WEST    AMIYA DASGUPTA
RUSSEL TITELMAN    LOWELL GEORGE
THE MERRY CLAYTON SINGERS    GENE PARSONS
BERNARD KRAUSER – moog synthesiser
NASSER RASTIGAR-NEJAD – santur

'Wake Up, Nigger' by the LAST POETS
Courtesy of Douglas Records
Buffy St Marie performed musically
through the courtesy of Vanguard Records.

*Camera tilts up jerkily from patchwork to Borges book and cover.*

associate producer   DAVID CAMMELL

*Close shot of Persian embroidered rug.*

film editors ANTONY GIBBS   BRIAN SMEDLEY-ASTON
art director   JOHN CLARK

*Freeze frame int. telephone box – Chas's doodle of the hanged man.*

production manager   ROBERT LYNN
assistant director   RICHARD BURGE
unit manager   KEVIN KAVANAGH
camera operator   MIKE MOLLOY
sound recordist   RON BARRON
sound editor   ALAN PATILLO
dialogue coach and
technical adviser   DAVID LITVINOFF
turner's house design
consultant   CHRISTOPHER GIBBS

*Close-up of Victorian slide of mountain range in Persia.*

set dresser   PETER YOUNG
continuity   ANABELLE DAVIS-GOFF
make-up   PAUL RABIGER
LINDA DE VETTA
hairdresser   HELEN LENNOX
wardrobe   EMMA PORTEOUS
BILLY JAY
costume consultant   DEBORAH DIXON

MR FOX'S SUITS by Hymie of Waterloo, London

*Victorian slide of Persian castle*

TECHNICOLOR

*Shot of Office Desk.*

Distributed by WARNER BROS

# APPENDIX
## The Opening Sequence.

FADE IN:

*Warner Brothers trademark.*

FADE OUT

   CUT TO BLACK

*Ground to air shot. Low-angle long shot of jet plane flying right to left. Camera pans with it and holds on sunburst.*

*Close shot jet engine, long shot vapour trail. Shot changes from day to night.*

EXT. COUNTRY ROAD – DAY

*Helicopter shot. Camera moving with black Rolls-Royce as it travels along road.*

SUPERIMPOSED TITLE JUMPS IN:

   A GOODTIMES ENTERPRISES PRODUCTION

SUPERIMPOSED TITLE JUMPS OUT

INT. CHAS'S FLAT – NIGHT

*High-angle medium-close shot, Chas's bottom moving top frame. Dana partially visible under him.*

EXT. COUNTRYSIDE – DAY

*Helicopter shot. Medium-long shot of black Rolls-Royce. Camera moves with car from left to right.*

INT. CHAS'S FLAT – NIGHT

*High-angle medium shot Dana, back to camera, lying on top of Chas. Camera tracks right to left and pans right to left.*

EXT. COUNTRYSIDE – DAY

*Helicopter shot. Medium-long shot. Camera moving left to right with black Rolls-Royce.*

JAMES FOX    MICK JAGGER

*Camera zooms out to long shot and moves left to right, panning round right to left as car travels foreground left.*

**SUPERIMPOSED TITLE JUMPS OUT**

*During this opening sequence, we hear Randy Newman's 'Gone Dead Train' on the soundtrack:*

> Shooting a supply from the demon's eye
> Instead of waiting for the time I hope I will
> Now the fire in the boiler up and quit before I came
> Ain't no empty cellar need a gone dead train
> Yes a gone dead train.

*Newman's song is followed by a moment of silence and then for the rest of the opening sequence we hear an eerie electronic music rising and falling like a whip.*

**INT. CHAS'S FLAT – NIGHT**

*High-angle close shot Dana's head moves right to reveal close shot of Chas's head. Hand-held camera follows movements as they roll about.*

*High-angle medium shot. Dana lying centre on bed. Chas's hands removing her panties. Chas then enters top of frame and lies of top of Dana. Hand-held camera tilts down with them.*

*High-angle close shot Dana and Chas making love. Hand-held camera pans right to left and down as they roll foreground.*

**EXT. COUNTRYSIDE – DAY**

*Helicopter shot. Long shot black Rolls-Royce travelling foreground, camera travelling back and panning right to left with it.*

**SUPERIMPOSED TITLE OVER:**

ANITA PALLENBERG

**SUPERIMPOSED TITLE AND BACKGROUND**

CUT TO:

INT. CHAS'S FLAT — NIGHT

*High-angle medium shot, Dana lying on top of Chas. Hand-held camera panning left to right as they roll right.*

*Shooting through reddish filter. High-angle close-up of Chas's face partially obscured by Dana's shoulder.*

EXT. COUNTRYSIDE — DAY

*Helicopter shot. Camera whip-panning left to right over trees to reveal the black Rolls-Royce in medium-long shot travelling foreground right. Camera travelling left to right with it.*

INT. CHAS'S FLAT — NIGHT

*High-angle medium-close shot Chas lying centre. Dana's head moves up and down rhythmically servicing him. Camera pans down.*

EXT. COUNTRYSIDE — DAY

*Helicopter shot. Medium-long shot black Rolls-Royce travelling foreground. Camera travelling back with it, then panning left to right as car exits foreground left.*

INT. CHAS'S FLAT — NIGHT

*High-angle medium-close shot. Dana's head between Chas's legs. Chas watching her intently in the mirror that he holds so as to get a clear view. Camera pans left to right and holds on mirror.*

SUPERIMPOSED TITLE JUMPS IN:

## PERFORMANCE

SUPERIMPOSED TITLE AND BACKGROUND CUT TO:

*High-angle close shot, Chas's hand holding mirror, medium-close shot Chas's reflection with Dana's head buried in his groin.*

EXT. COUNTRYSIDE — DAY

*Helicopter shot. Medium-long shot, camera tracking back with black Rolls-Royce as it drives foreground.*

INT. CHAS'S FLAT — NIGHT

*High-angle close shot Chas. Extreme close up Dana's head partially visible.*

*High-angle medium-close shot, Dana lying on bed. Chas partially visible sitting astride her and slapping her face.*

EXT. COUNTRYSIDE — DAY

*Low-angle medium shot Chauffeur driving Rolls-Royce left to right. Camera tracking with it and zooming into close shot of Chauffeur.*

INT. CHAS'S FLAT — NIGHT

*High-angle medium-close shot, Dana partially visible lying on bed, past medium-close shot, Chas's hands holding whip.*

EXT. COUNTRYSIDE — DAY

*Helicopter shot. Camera travelling left to right with black Rolls-Royce.*

INT. CHAS'S FLAT — NIGHT

*High-angle medium-close shot, Dana lying on bed reacting to Chas (out of shot).*

EXT. COUNTRYSIDE — DAY

*Helicopter shot. Medium shot, camera travelling left to right with black Rolls-Royce as it drives left to right.*

INT. CHAS'S FLAT — NIGHT

*High-angle medium-close shot of Dana lying centre on bed. Chas's hands holding whip around her throat.*

*High-angle medium-close shot, Chas and Dana locked in embrace and rolling about on bed. Hand-held camera following them.*

EXT. COUNTRYSIDE — DAY

*Medium shot, camera tracking back with Rolls-Royce as it drives foreground.*

INT. CHAS'S FLAT — NIGHT

*High-angle medium-close shot, Dana's hand grabbing Chas's back.*

EXT. COUNTRYSIDE – DAY

*Medium shot, camera tracking back with Rolls-Royce as it travels foreground.*

INT. CHAS'S FLAT – NIGHT

*High-angle medium-close shot, Dana's hand grabbing Chas's back.*

EXT. COUNTRYSIDE – DAY

*Medium shot, camera tracking back with Rolls-Royce as it travels foreground.*

INT. CHAS'S FLAT – NIGHT

*High-angle medium-close shot, Dana's hand grabbing Chas's back.*

EXT. COUNTRYSIDE – DAY

*Medium shot, camera whip-panning right to left over trees.*

INT. CHAS'S FLAT – NIGHT

*Medium-close shot, limbs locked together.*

EXT. COUNTRYSIDE – DAY

*Medium shot, camera whip-panning left to right over trees.*

INT. CHAS'S FLAT – NIGHT

*High-angle close shot, entangled limbs.*

EXT. COUNTRYSIDE – DAY

*Medium shot, camera whip-panning left to right over trees.*

INT. CHAS'S FLAT – NIGHT

*High-angle close shot, Chas's hand on Dana's body. Camera pans right to left as his hand moves left.*

EXT. COUNTRYSIDE – DAY

*Medium shot, camera whip-panning left to right over trees.*

INT. CHAS'S FLAT – NIGHT

*High-angle close shot, Chas's hand by Dana's breast. Camera pans right to left, losing hand.*

EXT. COUNTRYSIDE – DAY

*Medium shot, camera whip-panning right to left over trees.*

INT. CHAS'S FLAT – NIGHT

*Close shot, Dana's breast and arm.*

EXT. COUNTRYSIDE – DAY

*Medium shot Rolls-Royce.*

INT. CHAS'S FLAT – NIGHT

*High-angle medium-close shot, Chas's and Dana's bodies locked together.*

EXT. COUNTRYSIDE – DAY

*Medium shot, Rolls-Royce.*

INT. CHAS'S FLAT – NIGHT

*High-angle medium-close shot, Chas's and Dana's bodies locked in embrace.*

EXT. COUNTRYSIDE – DAY

*Medium shot, Rolls-Royce.*

INT. CHAS'S FLAT – NIGHT

*High-angle medium-close shot, Chas's and Dana's bodies locked in embrace.*

EXT. COUNTRYSIDE – DAY

*Medium shot, Rolls-Royce.*

INT. CHAS'S FLAT – NIGHT

*High-angle medium-close shot, Chas's and Dana's bodies locked in embrace.*

EXT. COUNTRYSIDE – DAY

*Medium shot, Rolls-Royce.*

INT. CHAS'S FLAT – NIGHT

*High-angle medium-close shot, Chas's and Dana's bodies locked in embrace.*

EXT. COUNTRYSIDE – DAY

*Medium shot, Rolls-Royce.*

INT. CHAS'S FLAT – NIGHT

*High-angle medium-close shot, Chas's and Dana's bodies locked in embrace.*

EXT. COUNTRYSIDE – DAY

*Medium shot, Rolls-Royce.*

INT. CHAS'S FLAT – NIGHT

*High-angle medium-close shot, Chas's and Dana's bodies locked in embrace.*

EXT. COUNTRYSIDE – DAY

*Medium shot, Rolls-Royce.*

INT. CHAS'S FLAT – NIGHT

*High-angle medium-close shot, Chas's and Dana's bodies locked in embrace.*

EXT. COUNTRYSIDE – DAY

*Medium shot, Rolls-Royce.*

INT. CHAS'S FLAT – NIGHT

*High-angle medium-close shot, Chas's bottom, Dana's hands clasped over it.*

EXT. COUNTRYSIDE – DAY

*Medium-long shot, Rolls-Royce, side view.*

INT. CHAS'S FLAT – NIGHT

*High-angle medium-close shot, Chas's bottom, Dana's hands clasped over it.*

EXT. COUNTRYSIDE – DAY

*Medium-long shot, Rolls-Royce, side view.*

INT. CHAS'S FLAT – NIGHT

*High-angle medium-close shot, Chas's bottom with Dana's hands clutching at it.*

137

EXT. COUNTRYSIDE – DAY

*Medium-long shot, Rolls-Royce, side view.*

INT. CHAS'S FLAT – NIGHT

*High-angle medium-close shot, Chas's bottom with Dana's hands clutching at it.*

EXT. COUNTRYSIDE – DAY

*Medium-long shot, Rolls-Royce, side view.*

INT. CHAS'S FLAT – NIGHT

*High-angle medium-close shot, Chas's bottom with Dana's fingernails digging into it.*

EXT. COUNTRYSIDE – DAY

*Medium-long shot, Rolls-Royce, side view.*

INT. CHAS'S FLAT – NIGHT

*High-angle medium-close shot, Chas's bottom with Dana's fingernails digging into it.*

EXT. COUNTRYSIDE – DAY

*Medium-long shot, Rolls-Royce, side view.*

INT. CHAS'S FLAT – NIGHT

*High-angle medium-close shot, Chas's bottom with Dana's fingernails digging into it.*

EXT. COUNTRYSIDE – DAY

*Medium-long shot, Rolls-Royce, partially hidden by vegetation.*

INT. CHAS'S FLAT – NIGHT

*High-angle medium-close shot, Chas's bottom with Dana's fingernails digging into it.*

EXT. COUNTRYSIDE – DAY

*Medium-long shot, Rolls-Royce, partially hidden by vegetation.*

INT. CHAS'S FLAT – NIGHT

*High-angle medium-close shot, Chas's bottom with Dana's fingernails digging into it.*

EXT. COUNTRYSIDE – DAY

*Medium-long shot, Rolls-Royce, side view.*

INT. CHAS'S FLAT – NIGHT

*High-angle medium-close shot, Chas's bottom with Dana's fingernails digging into it.*

EXT. COUNTRYSIDE – DAY

*Medium-long shot, Rolls-Royce.*

INT. CHAS'S FLAT – NIGHT

*High-angle medium-close shot, Chas's bottom with Dana's fingernails digging into it.*

EXT. PUB – DAY

*Long shot of Rolls-Royce driving from background centre to foreground left. Camera zooms in to close-up of blacked-out rear window.*

INT. CHAS'S FLAT – NIGHT

*High-angle close shot, Dana's breast and arm. Camera tilts up as she sits up.*

EXT. PUB – DAY

*Medium-long shot of Rolls-Royce driving foreground left. Camera zooms in to close-up of blacked-out rear window.*

INT. CHAS'S FLAT – NIGHT

*Close-up, Dana, right, holding sheet to her mouth, facing left. She lowers it and picks up Chas's hand from out of shot and then bites it.*

EXT. PUB – DAY

*Close shot, Chauffeur eating pie. Camera pans down left to right as he leans right, then zooms out to reveal him cleaning car.*

INT. CHAS'S FLAT – DAY

*Close-up of Chas rubbing eyes. Camera tracks back to medium-close shot. Medium-close shot of photographs on wall past half-open door. Camera tracks right to left as door closes.*

EXT. PUB – DAY

*Hand resting on arm rest in car, past medium-close shot of Chauffeur closing car door.*

INT. CHAS'S FLAT – DAY

*High-angle medium-close shot of tray with Chas's money, watch, pen etc. laid neatly on it. High-angle close shot, Dana. Camera tilts up to bedclothes, losing her. Medium shot, camera tilting up to reveal Chas and Dana asleep in bed.*

EXT. PUB – DAY

*Medium-close shot, electric window in Rolls-Royce closing. Camera tilting up with it and holds as car drives left.*